The

5-Minute

BIBLE STUDY

for the

Anxious Heart

Member of the
Evangelical Christian
Publishers Association

The
5-Minute
BIBLE
STUDY

for the

Anxious
Heart

JANICE THOMPSON

BARBOUR BOOKS
An Imprint of Barbour Publishing, Inc.

INTRODUCTION

Are you struggling with anxiety? Do life's cares overwhelm you at times? This Bible study was designed with you in mind. It provides an avenue for you to open the Bible regularly and dig into a passage—even if you only have five minutes!

Here's how the study works:

- Minutes 1–2: *Read* carefully the scripture passage for each Bible study.
- Minute 3: *Understand.* Ponder a couple of prompts designed to help you apply the verses from the Bible to your own life.
- Minute 4: *Apply.* Read a brief devotion based on the day's scripture. Think about how to apply the scriptural truths to your own life.
- Minute 5: *Pray.* A prayer starter will help you begin a time of conversation with God. Remember to allow time for Him to speak into your life as well.

May *The 5-Minute Bible Study for the Anxious Heart* help you establish the discipline of studying God's Word. Pour yourself a cup of coffee and make that first five minutes of your day count! You will find that even a few minutes focused on scripture and prayer has the power to make a huge difference. Soon you will see those anxieties fading away, replaced with overwhelming faith.

HE ALWAYS KNEW YOU
Read Jeremiah 1

⌒

Key Verse:

*"Before I formed you in the womb I knew you,
before you were born I set you apart; I appointed
you as a prophet to the nations."*
JEREMIAH 1:5 NIV

Understand:

- *If God knew you before you were born, He
  must have carefully selected the location and
  year of your birth as well. What if you had
  been born a hundred years sooner?*
- *God set you apart to do great things. What
  does that mean to you? What great things do
  you hope to accomplish?*

Apply:

As you ponder the story of Jeremiah, as you think
about how God called him into ministry, think of
your own life. Consider the notion that the Creator
of the universe knew you before you were born. He
was there all along, carefully choosing your parents,
your place of birth, even the year you would enter
the world.

When you take the time to truly analyze these
things, it's easy to see how special you are to God.
He cared enough about you, even before birth, to

plot out your entrance to the planet. He could have chosen any time, any place, but He knew just when to drop you onto the scene so that you could have the greatest impact for the kingdom of God. Wow!

God is at work, even now. Can you feel the anticipation stirring in your heart? He's got amazing things for you. Sure, there will still be a few bumps and bruises along the way. The road ahead will be filled with twists and turns, but He will guide you (and use you) every step of the way. So lay down those anxieties and take His hand. He's got this!

Pray:

Father, thank You for arranging the details of my life.
It amazes me to think that You chose my parents, my lineage,
my hair color, my personality, and so on. I'm also tickled
to think that You chose for me to be born in the very year
I was born, and in the very location I was born.
Wow, Lord! You've covered it all. Amen.

....

....

....

....

....

....

....

....

GOD'S REPLACEMENT POLICY
Read Acts 9:1–31

⌒

Key Verse:

Immediately, something like scales fell from Saul's eyes, and he could see again. He got up and was baptized, and after taking some food, he regained his strength.
ACTS 9:18–19 NIV

Understand:

- *Have you ever walked through a season where you felt like you had scales on your eyes and couldn't see clearly? How did you make it through?*
- *If you've walked through seasons of rebellion, what finally drew you back to God? Are you motivated more by fear or love?*

Apply:

Saul was simply walking down the road, minding his own business, when God interrupted his life and brought lasting change. Maybe you've been there too. Maybe you lived your life your own way, according to your own terms, not caring what anyone else thought. Then God ripped the scales from your eyes and gave you brand-new vision to see things as He does. Amazing!

If you've ever experienced a radical transformation like that, then you can surely relate to Saul's journey. Out with the old, in with the new! God has a great replacement policy. He wants to take your old, broken life—the one riddled with worries, cares, and woes—and replace it with a new, whole one. He wants to point you in the right direction and win your heart. What an amazing and loving God He is.

Pray:

Lord, thank You for Your transformative power! I'm so grateful You've intervened in my life and given me a second chance. I choose to live my life for You, Father. Amen.

....

....

....

....

....

....

....

....

....

....

....

....

....

SUPERNATURAL PEACE
Read Acts 16:16–40

⁓

Key Verse:

About midnight Paul and Silas were praying and singing hymns to God, and the other prisoners were listening to them. Suddenly there was such a violent earthquake that the foundations of the prison were shaken. At once all the prison doors flew open, and everyone's chains came loose.
ACTS 16:25–26 NIV

Understand:

- *Maybe you're like Paul and Silas. Maybe you've been through a situation where you were falsely accused or held accountable for something you weren't responsible for. How did God come to your rescue? Did He give you peace in the middle of the situation?*
- *Worship plays a major role in breaking free from the past. How has God used songs of praise to encourage your heart?*

Apply:

Don't you love this story of what happened to Paul and Silas while in prison? Perhaps you're struck by the fact that they were singing worship songs to God—right there, behind prison bars. (It takes a lot of faith to worship your way through a tough situation, doesn't it?) These men were seemingly undeterred by their plight as they lifted their voices in a mighty chorus to the Lord.

What God did next was rather astounding! He shook the earth, rattled their chains, threw open the doors, and released them from their imprisonment. Wow!

But you rarely hear of a prison story ending like this. Paul and Silas could have run for the hills. Instead, they took the time to minister to their jailer and lead him to the Lord. What an amazing night that must have been!

Pray:

Lord, thank You for the reminder that I can praise my way through the darkest night. When I lift a song to You, anxieties have to go! Even when I'm feeling trapped or imprisoned by a situation, You give me a song of praise. I'm so grateful. Amen.

....

....

....

....

....

....

....

....

REBUILDING THE WALLS
Read Nehemiah 2:11–20

Key Verse:

I also told them about the gracious hand of my God on me and what the king had said to me. They replied, "Let us start rebuilding." So they began this good work.
NEHEMIAH 2:18 NIV

Understand:

- *Are there places in your life that feel broken down or irreparable? What lessons can you learn from Nehemiah so that rebuilding can begin to take place?*
- *God loves you so much that He wants to bring beauty from ashes, fortification from rubble. Can you begin to trust Him today, so that rebuilding can begin?*

Apply:

Nehemiah's heart nearly twisted in two as he looked out over the rubble in Jerusalem. Maybe you can relate. You've been through good seasons, where the walls stood firm, and then you watched them crumble to the ground around you. Now your stomach is in knots, and you wonder if you'll ever feel normal again.

When you're in the middle of a "walls have fallen down" season, it's hard to know where to begin to pick up the pieces. Anxieties can get the best of you. Follow Nehemiah's lead. He started by acknowledging the situation; then he gathered teams to begin the rebuilding process. He laid out a plan for success.

That's what God wants for you too. Begin to strategize. You can move forward. You will overcome. These worries will soon fade, replaced by hope and peace.

Surround yourself with godly friends; then begin the process of rebuilding.

Pray:

Lord, I submit myself to the process of rebuilding. I know it won't be easy, but You're a miracle-working God, and I know You can bring beauty from ashes. I praise You in advance and anticipate what You will do. Amen.

....

....

....

....

....

....

....

....

....

LIVE FOR TODAY
Read Genesis 19:15-26

Key Verse:

But Lot's wife looked back, and she became a pillar of salt.
GENESIS 19:26 NIV

Understand:

- *Like Lot's wife, you've probably been tempted to look back a time or two. Think of a particular time when God instructed you to move forward, but you felt tempted to glance back over your shoulder.*
- *What's the most precarious situation God has delivered you from? Aren't you glad you don't have to go back to that?*

Apply:

My goodness, Lot went through a *lot*. When it came time for him to leave Sodom and Gomorrah, God gave him specific instructions. He was not to look back. No gazing at the past. Unfortunately, his wife disobeyed God's commands and turned back for one last glance. She paid the ultimate price with her life.

Maybe you've been there. Maybe you've camped out in a place of unbelief and surrounded yourself with people who encouraged you to live the wrong way. You've done your time in Sodom and Gomorrah. But now you have regrets. You want out. God has a way of pulling you out of such places and seasons. When He does, you can count on Him to say, *"Don't look back." "Don't let the past define you." "Live for today."*

Take heart! There are better days ahead. Just keep looking forward and putting one foot in front of the other. And, whatever you do, don't be tempted to glance back over your shoulder.

Pray:

Lord, I'm so glad my days of sin and rebellion are behind me. Thank You for delivering me! I'm so grateful for a happy road ahead. With Your help, I won't look back. Amen.

....

....

....

....

....

....

....

....

....

....

....

DON'T LOOK DOWN
Read Matthew 14:22–33

Key Verse:

"Lord, if it's you," Peter replied, "tell me to come to you on the water." "Come," he said. Then Peter got down out of the boat, walked on the water and came toward Jesus. But when he saw the wind, he was afraid and, beginning to sink, cried out, "Lord, save me!" Immediately Jesus reached out his hand and caught him. "You of little faith," he said, "why did you doubt?"
MATTHEW 14:28–31 NIV

Understand:

- *Some situations in life require extraordinary faith and courage—total focus on God. Think of a time when God asked you to get out of the proverbial boat and walk in faith. Did you think you would survive?*
- *What a bold move on Peter's part, to take that first step! Think of your most courageous move to date. How did God honor your courage and faithfulness?*

Apply:

There are so many fascinating details in this story. Don't you find it intriguing that Peter says, "Lord, if it's You, tell me to come to You." How many times do we do that? "Lord, if You're really asking me to take this job, send me a sign." "Lord, if it's really You asking me to provide groceries for that family in need, give me a nudge." "Lord, if You want me to date this person, have him call me on the phone."

The key thing is, Peter got out of the boat. His heart was in the right place and his faith was high. . . until he took his eyes off Jesus. That happens to us too. We move forward, convinced we'll make it through, and then we get distracted with the cares of life. Oops! Down we go. Fear and anxiety cripple us and cause us to sink.

What's distracting you today? What can you do to better keep your eyes on Jesus? Wherever you're headed, just remember one thing: don't look down. Keep your eyes on Him.

Pray:

Lord, thank You for the reminder that I can walk in faith as long as I stay completely focused on You. I'm ready to be rid of my anxieties and fears. Please help me, I pray. Amen.

....

....

....

....

....

....

....

THE MOST UNLIKELY ONE
Read 1 Samuel 16:1–13

~

Key Verse:

So he asked Jesse, "Are these all the sons you have?" "There is still the youngest," Jesse answered. "He is tending the sheep." Samuel said, "Send for him; we will not sit down until he arrives." So he sent for him and had him brought in. He was glowing with health and had a fine appearance and handsome features. Then the LORD said, "Rise and anoint him; this is the one."
1 SAMUEL 16:11–12 NIV

Understand:

- *God's ways are not our ways. Sometimes He chooses the most unlikely person. Have you ever been that person? If so, how did He call you out of your comfort zone?*
- *It's not always easy to submit to the authority of someone younger than yourself. Have you ever been in a situation (on the job or at church) where someone younger took a position of leadership? If so, how did you respond?*

Apply:

Think of young David, the shepherd boy, tending sheep in the field. Just an ordinary day. Nothing big on the horizon.

Enter Samuel, the man appointed by God to seek out the future king. David could not have known that Samuel would point a finger in his direction and say, "Him! He's the one." David was, after all, just a boy. And just a lowly shepherd at that.

Aren't you glad God looks at the heart, not outward appearance? If He judged based on human criteria, David would never have made the cut.

God wants to use the ordinary people of this world to do extraordinary things. His ways are not our ways. But don't be surprised when He interrupts your run-of-the-mill day to call you to that next big task. But no worries. Push those anxieties aside! If He calls, He will equip. So hang on to your hat. There are big things ahead!

Pray:

Lord, I don't know what You have for my future, but I know I can trust You. There are days when I feel like David—lowly and plain. But I know You have big things ahead for me. I wait with expectancy, Father! Amen.

....

....

....

....

....

....

....

AS YOU SAY, LORD
Read Luke 1:26–38

⁓

Key Verse:

Mary said, "I am the servant of the Lord. Let this happen to me as you say!" Then the angel went away.
LUKE 1:38 NCV

Understand:

- *Perhaps the most famous words spoken by Mary were these: "Let this happen to me as you say!" What courage and faith that response must have taken! Have you ever walked through a season where you had to "let go and let God" as Mary did? Were you able to say: "Let this happen to me as You say, Lord!"?*

- *Does your anxiety ever get the best of you when God calls you out of your comfort zone? How do you cope?*

Apply:

Can you even imagine walking in Mary's shoes? The stress, the anxiety of having to play such a tremendous role in God's story must have seemed overwhelming at times. What a task for such a young woman!

Mary's response is one we can all learn from: "Let this happen to me as you say!" Those aren't easy words to speak, especially when you're going through

rough stuff. More often we pray, "Lord, lift this burden!" or "Lord, please bring instantaneous healing." The quicker we can shake off the stress, the better. Rarely do we say, "Let it be done unto me as You see fit, Lord."

Oh, but if only we could! There's so much to learn from Mary's journey. She saw it through from beginning to end, and she embraced God's plan with her whole heart—from the cradle to the cross.

Pray:

Lord, I don't always want to utter the words "As You wish, Lord." More often, I want to say, "Please get me out of this mess so that the knots in my stomach can come untied." But today I choose to submit to Your plan for my life. May I, like Mary, sync my heart to Yours so that Your perfect will is done in my life. Amen.

....

....

....

....

....

....

....

....

....

DO IT GOD'S WAY
Read Genesis 16:1–15

⌒

Key Verse:

*So after Abram had been living in Canaan ten years,
Sarai his wife took her Egyptian slave Hagar
and gave her to her husband to be his wife.*
GENESIS 16:3 NIV

Understand:

- *Sometimes, when our anxieties are high and
our faith is low, we step out on our own and
take matters into our own hands. Have you
ever done that? How did it work out?*
- *Who was most to blame in this situation—
Abraham, Sarah, or Hagar? Have you ever
been in a situation where everyone involved
got ahead of God?*

Apply:

It doesn't take much effort to see that Sarah got ahead
of God in this twisted tale. When she saw that she
could not provide a child for her husband, she went
to her maid and concocted a plan to keep Abraham's
lineage going. Can you even imagine Hagar's shock
at Sarah's suggestion?

Now picture the jealousies that surely arose
when Hagar's son, Ishmael, was born. Sarah, the very
one who came up with the plan, was riddled with

jealousy. If she had just waited, if she hadn't jumped the gun, she would have seen the fruition of God's plan in her own life. She should have waited on Isaac.

Maybe you know what it's like to get antsy, to feel like you need to come up with your own plan because God isn't moving fast enough to suit you. You let your fears and anxieties get the better of you. Anytime you do that, you're stepping out from under the umbrella of His protection and safety. It's better to hang on to your faith and believe that He will come through for you, even if circumstances make you feel otherwise.

Pray:

Lord, I don't want to get ahead of You! I don't want to take off down the road, thinking I've found a better way. Stop me in my tracks, I pray. Quiet my heart. May I stick close to You and trust in Your plan. Amen.

....

....

....

....

....

....

....

....

....

WITH THANKSGIVING
Read John 5:1–13

~

Key Verse:

*Jesus told him, "Stand up, pick up
your mat, and walk!"*
JOHN 5:8 NLT

Understand:

- *Life presents many situations where you
  simply feel stuck. You see no way out. Think of
  a time when you wondered if your situation
  would ever change. How did God redeem
  that situation?*
- *Has the Lord ever spoken so clearly that you
  could almost hear Him say, "Get up and move
  on!"? If so, did you do as He said?*

Apply:

When you're reclining at the pool of Bethesda, wait-ing on your miracle, the days start running together. After a while, you start to wonder if the long-awaited healing will ever take place. Then, on a day when you least expect it, Jesus shows up! He utters a few simple words: *"Stand up, pick up your mat, and walk!"* and you stare at Him, wanting to ask the obvious question: "How?"

But you do it. When the Savior tells you to walk, you walk! So you stand, legs shaky at first, unaccustomed to being used. But there's no pain, no stiffness, no atrophy. . .nothing! It makes no sense, but before you know it you're leaping and dancing and praising the Lord for intervening in your life. Thanksgiving and praise become your song of choice, replacing the "woe is me" ballad you've crooned for so long.

Can you relate to the story? Surely you've been through seasons of unexpected blessing, healing, and joy. All you can do is lift your voice in praise to the Savior!

Pray:

Thank You, Lord, for showing up when You do. I never know when. I never know how. I only know that You will. . .because You said You would. I want to lift my voice in praise for Your intervention, Lord. Amen!

....

....

....

....

....

....

....

....

....

THE HEM OF HIS GARMENT
Read Matthew 9:18–34

⁓

Key Verse:

Just then a woman who had been subject to bleeding for twelve years came up behind him and touched the edge of his cloak. She said to herself, "If I only touch his cloak, I will be healed."
MATTHEW 9:20–21 NIV

Understand:

- *Have you ever been through a particularly hard health battle, one you were afraid would never end? How did it affect your faith? Were you anxious?*
- *When you think of the woman pushing her way through the crowd of people to get to Jesus, what images come to mind? Have you ever pushed through a situation to get to the Lord?*

Apply:

Twelve years. She waited twelve long years for her miracle. Years of being ostracized and an outcast. Years of painful, embarrassing bleeding. Twelve years of not being welcome at social events or get-togethers.

And then, in a moment of desperation, she came up with a plan: push through the crowd. Grab the hem of Jesus' garment. Pray for a miracle. With desperation leading the way, she did just that, and eventually she landed at Jesus' feet, arm outstretched as she grabbed hold of the fabric on His cloak.

Can you relate to this woman? Have you ever been so desperate to see God move in your life that you would press through any circumstance, risk ridicule or jeering, just to get to Him? God honors that sort of desperation. He longs to see His kids healed and whole, their anxieties a thing of the past. So go on! What's holding you back? Press through the crowd and stretch your arm in His direction. God's got big things planned for you!

Pray:

Father, thank You for the many times You've answered my prayers of desperation. I know You will never cast me aside, Lord. What a good, loving Father You are. Amen.

....

....

....

....

....

....

....

....

....

REBORN!
Read John 3:1–21

⌒

Key Verse:

*"You should not be surprised at my saying,
'You must be born again.'"*
JOHN 3:7 NIV

Understand:

- *It's impossible to remember your own physical birth, but do you have a memory of the day you gave your heart to the Lord? What was that day like?*
- *When you explain the salvation process to others, do you share from your own journey? What do you say?*

Apply:

Countless Bible stories tell tales of men and women who messed up and wanted to start over. Thank goodness God is in the do-over business. He loves to offer second chances.

There's one do-over that outshines every other, and it's found in one little word: *salvation.* When we accept Jesus Christ as Lord and Savior, when we step into relationship with Him, we are reborn.

Think about that prefix "re-" for a moment. It means "again." When we accept Jesus, we're born. . . again. We get a do-over. A big one! Gone are the mistakes of the past. Washed away are our sins. Gone are the worries about who we used to be. In place of all these things, a clean slate. What an amazing gift from our Father, God!

Pray:

Thank You, Lord, for offering me new life in You. I've been born again, Father! My heart now belongs to You. I can hardly wait to get started on this journey together. Amen.

....

....

....

....

....

....

....

....

....

....

....

....

....

....

HOME AT LAST
Read Luke 15:11–32

⌒

Key Verse:

" 'Bring the fattened calf and kill it. Let's have a feast and celebrate. For this son of mine was dead and is alive again; he was lost and is found.' So they began to celebrate."
LUKE 15:23–24 NIV

Understand:

- *Has your family ever dealt with a prodigal? If so, how did it affect the family's spiritual health?*
- *Think of a time in your life when you wandered from the Lord. How far did you get before He wooed you back home again?*

Apply:

Perhaps no other story in the Bible has touched the hearts of believers like the tale of the prodigal son. Many relate because they have lived the life of a wanderer. Still others relate because they feel like the older brother.

Regardless of where you find yourself in the story, the outcome is the same: God loves His kids and won't give up on them. He longs for every wandering, broken, anxious heart to turn itself back toward home, for sin and separation to be a thing of the past.

What are you struggling with today? Do you feel like you've wandered too far? Are you, like the older brother, dealing with a judgmental spirit or jealousy? Regardless, God wants to completely heal you, make you whole, and sweep you back into the fold. You are His child, and He adores you.

Pray:

You're the best Dad ever! No matter how far I stray, no matter how badly I fumble, You're standing there, arms wide open, to welcome me back home. How can I ever thank You, Lord? My heart is filled with praise. Amen.

....
....
....
....
....
....
....
....
....
....
....
....

PARTING THE SEA
Read Exodus 14

⌣

Key Verse:

Then Moses put out his hand over the sea. And the Lord moved the sea all night by a strong east wind. So the waters were divided.
EXODUS 14:21 NLV

Understand:

- *God moved in a mighty way to protect His children when He parted the Red Sea. What miracles has He performed on your behalf?*
- *When was the last time you faced a situation that seemed impassable, like Israel and the Red Sea? How did you make it through?*

Apply:

Talk about an epic scene! This is one for the history books, filled with all the excitement and drama of a Hollywood movie. Picture the Israelites, on a trek out of Egypt across the desert. Enter Pharaoh's army, on the move to stop the Israelites in their tracks.

The Israelites come to the edge of the Red Sea. They're trapped, sick with worry and anxiety. There's no way across—no boats, no bridges, nothing. They're trapped, and the enemy is gaining ground. Surely all is about to be lost.

Then, in an astounding move, God pushes back

the water. The Israelites pass through on dry land. Their enemy presses in hard behind them. . .and the waters rush over Pharaoh's army, killing them all.

This story of God's miraculous protection of His children should fill your heart with hope. If He was willing to change nature for the Hebrew children, what will He do for you?

Pray:

Lord, what a story! I wish I'd been there in person to witness the parting of the sea firsthand. Thank You for protecting Your children, both then and now. I'm so grateful Your protective hand is at work in my life. Amen.

....

....

....

....

....

....

....

....

....

....

....

....

IT'S A CHOICE
Read Luke 10:25–37

~

Key Verse:

"Which of these three do you think was a neighbor to the man who fell into the hands of robbers?" The expert in the law replied, "The one who had mercy on him." Jesus told him, "Go and do likewise."
LUKE 10:36–37 NIV

Understand:

- *When you read the story of the Good Samaritan, which character do you most relate to—the one in need, the one passing by, or the one stopping to offer help?*
- *Think of a time when a Good Samaritan intervened in your life. How did the actions of this person change the outcome of your situation?*

Apply:

Likely you've known this story from childhood—the tale of the Good Samaritan caring for the man in need on the side of the road. Maybe you've skimmed over the story, convinced it has nothing to do with your current reality.

Then you pass by a coworker in her cubicle. She's crying because she's in an abusive marriage and doesn't know what to do.

Or you drive by a man on the street corner, begging for food. He's exhausted. Overheated. Completely defeated by life.

Or maybe you receive a call from a friend, riddled with anxiety because her child has wandered away from the Lord.

The truth is, life gives us many opportunities to play the role of Good Samaritan. Whether you're working at the church's food pantry, volunteering to coach at the neighborhood Little League, or letting a friend cry on your shoulder, you've got what it takes to minister to others. And God is very, very proud of the work you are doing.

Pray:

Lord, I don't often feel like I'm doing enough to help others. Show me ways to touch those who are hurting. May I, like the Good Samaritan, really make a difference in someone's life today. Amen.

....

....

....

....

....

....

....

THE BURNING BUSH
Read Exodus 3:1–17

Key Verse:

*"Do not come any closer," God said. "Take off your sandals,
for the place where you are standing is holy ground."*
EXODUS 3:5 NIV

Understand:

- *Think of a time when you truly felt like you
  were in God's presence. What did it feel like?*
- *Picture yourself in Moses' sandals. What
  might he have thought as the Lord spoke to
  him through the burning bush?*

Apply:

When you're walking through a stressful season and
you're looking for the perfect place to calm your
nerves, the very safest (and most peaceful) place is
the presence of God. When you cross over the invisible
line into the holy of holies, everything else disappears.
Worries cease. Cares flee. Troubles vanish. All
the things that have kept your stomach in knots have
to go in His presence.

What's troubling you today? Can you, like
Moses, stand in front of the burning bush and let go
of the things that have held you in their grasp? Can
you toss them into His fiery presence and see them
consumed? God longs for you to live in peace, and

your first step toward finding peace is getting into God's presence.

What's holding you back? Take off those sandals and run into His holy presence today.

Pray:

Lord, today I choose to spend quality time with You. I let go of my fears, my troubles, my anxieties. I place my hand in Yours and cross—feet bare—into Your holy presence. Thank You for what You're doing in my life, Lord. Amen.

....

....

....

....

....

....

....

....

....

....

....

....

....

HERE AM I. . .SEND ME
Read Isaiah 6:1–8

⌒

Key Verse:

*Then I heard the voice of the Lord, saying,
"Whom shall I send, and who will go for Us?"
Then I said, "Here am I. Send me!"*
ISAIAH 6:8 NASB

Understand:

- *Can you remember a time in your life when
  the Lord specifically called you to go someplace
  out of your comfort zone? Did you hide in
  fear or respond, like Isaiah, "Here am I. Send
  me!"?*
- *When was the last time you felt the Lord
  nudge you to do something difficult or
  unusual?*

Apply:

Isaiah found himself in an amazing position, didn't
he? When the Lord asked the question *"Whom shall
I send, and who will go for Us?"* Isaiah was faced with
a choice—to stay or to go. With no hesitation, he
responded, "Here am I. Send me!"

If you've ever spent time in God's presence, really
drawing close to Him, perhaps you've had those little
nudges. Maybe you've heard God whisper to your
heart, *"Go here,"* or *"Do this"* or *"Do that."* When the

almighty Author of the universe speaks, how do you respond? Ideally, like Isaiah!

If God reveals something to you during your quiet time with Him, don't be afraid. Simply raise your hand and say, "I'm here, Lord. I hear You, and I'm willing to go." But don't be surprised where He sends you once you've said it! Your journey is about to get really interesting!

Pray:

Lord, here am I. Send me. Send me to my friends, that I might be a witness. Send me to my coworkers, that I might show compassion. Send me wherever You choose, that I might shine brightly for You. Amen.

....

....

....

....

....

....

....

....

....

....

....

GIFTED TO SERVE
Read 1 Corinthians 12

Key Verse:

*Now to each one the manifestation of the
Spirit is given for the common good.*
1 CORINTHIANS 12:7 NIV

Understand:

- *When you look over the list of spiritual gifts,
  which ones stand out to you? Why?*
- *Is there an area of your life where you excel?
  What is your strongest gift, and how have
  you used it?*

Apply:

If you've ever done a Bible study of the spiritual gifts,
then it's likely you've taken a test to see which ones
you possess.

Which gifts are your strongest? Are you called
to minister through words of wisdom or knowledge?
Do you have a prophetic gifting or the ability to pray
for healing? There are so many ways to reach out to
others using these gifts.

When you realize that God is the One working
through you—that you don't have to figure it out on
your own—then your anxieties are squashed. There's
no need to fret. God's got this.

Open your heart to be used by God in the gifts

of the Spirit; then watch as He touches others in a supernatural way. . .through you.

Lord, how amazing! You've given me gifts to be used to reach others. Today I lay down my fears, my concerns, and choose to operate in those gifts, Lord. Use me, I pray. Amen.

....

....

....

....

....

....

....

....

....

....

....

....

....

....

....

....

MANNA
Read Exodus 16

⌒

Key Verse:

Then the LORD said to Moses, "I will rain down bread from heaven for you. The people are to go out each day and gather enough for that day. In this way I will test them and see whether they will follow my instructions."
EXODUS 16:4 NIV

Understand:

- *God is in the "providing" business. The Bible promises that He will take care of His kids. Think of a particular time when God came through for you, pouring down unexpected manna.*
- *How can you be a manna provider for others in need?*

Apply:

We often say, "Lord, I don't need much. Just give me what I need, not what I want." Likely, the Israelites prayed that too. "Lord, just a little food will suffice to see us through." Then, manna fell like a feast from the skies. At first the Hebrew children were thrilled to have it. Then, after a while, it wasn't so tasty. They grew tired of it.

What an amazing story this would have been if the Israelites continued to praise and thank God for

His provision instead of grumbling. If only they could have seen manna as a blessing instead of drudgery.

Maybe you can relate. What felt like a blessing in the beginning is now part of your everyday humdrum existence. You've forgotten to be thankful. The mortgage gets paid, and you don't remember to thank God. The electric bill is paid, and you let it pass by like it's nothing.

Every day God is blessing you. Don't forget to stop and thank Him for the manna!

Pray:

Lord, thank You for the many times and ways You have provided for me. Show me how to be a blessing to others, I pray. I want to be one who provides manna (refreshment, nourishment) to those You place in my path. Amen.

....

....

....

....

....

....

....

....

....

....

HE'S GOT YOU COVERED
Read Ruth 3

~

Key Verse:

*"Wash, put on perfume, and get dressed in your best clothes.
Then go down to the threshing floor, but don't let him know
you are there until he has finished eating and drinking.
When he lies down, note the place where he is lying.
Then go and uncover his feet and lie down.
He will tell you what to do."*
RUTH 3:3–4 NIV

Understand:

- *Through good times and bad, God's got you
  covered. Think of a time when He proved this
  to you.*
- *Has anxiety ever left you feeling vulnerable?
  How did God cover or protect you during this
  vulnerable season?*

Apply:

The story of Ruth and Boaz is one that brings great
hope to those who feel lost and alone. Precious Ruth
lost her husband at a young age. Her mother-in-law,
Naomi, slipped into the role of mentor and friend.
The two became so close that Ruth clung to the
older woman, even returning to Naomi's homeland
with her after the family tragedy.

When push came to shove in Ruth's life, she

continued to look to Naomi for advice. Through Naomi, she eventually found her husband-to-be, Boaz, a man who swept her into his fold and covered her with the edge of his robe.

Do you have a Naomi or Boaz in your life? Who covers you, shields you when you're vulnerable? Have you become that person for others? Perhaps there's a friend, mentor, family member, or coworker who shares her thoughts with you. Or, maybe you've become a Naomi to a younger woman in your world.

This special bond between younger woman and older is so precious. God wants all His girls—regardless of age—to learn from one another and to grow in the faith as their friendships grow as well.

Pray:

Lord, thank You for placing godly women in my life—women I can learn from, bounce ideas off of, and share personal concerns with. It's difficult to be anxious with so many friends cheering me on. I'm so grateful for them, Lord. Amen.

....

....

....

....

....

....

THE WATER'S EDGE
Read Psalm 23

Key Verse:

He makes me lie down in green pastures, he leads me beside quiet waters, he refreshes my soul. He guides me along the right paths for his name's sake.
PSALM 23:2–3 NIV

Understand:

- *Have you ever walked through a season where the Lord specifically instructed you to rest, to lie in green pastures beside still waters?*
- *What's the hardest thing about resting for you?*

Apply:

He leads me beside still waters. How many times have you quoted those words? But have you ever paused to consider their meaning? When God leads us beside still waters, He's drawing us away from the cares and anxieties of life, far from the busyness, the harried schedule, the pressures of the day. At the water's edge, life is calm, still. The only things moving are the wind whispering through the trees and the gentle waters of the brook below.

He leads me beside still waters. . .so that I can rest my mind. Stop my crazy thoughts from tumbling through my brain. Quiet my heart.

He leads me beside still waters. . .so that my soul can be restored, my joy replenished, my hope resurrected.

He leads me beside still waters so that anxieties will cease.

Today, allow the Lord to take you by the hand and lead you beside still waters. You'll find all you need and more.

Pray:

Father, thank You for drawing me away from the chaos and the pain to a peaceful place with You. I willingly follow You to the still waters, that I might find peace. Amen.

....

....

....

....

....

....

....

....

....

....

....

....

REBUKE THE WAVES
Read Mark 4:35–41

Key Verse:

He got up and spoke sharp words to the wind. He said to the sea, "Be quiet! Be still." At once the wind stopped blowing. There were no more waves.
MARK 4:39 NLV

Understand:

- *Life presents unexpected storms sometimes. Think of one that caught you off guard. How did Jesus calm the storm?*
- *What role can you play as a storm calmer in the lives of others?*

Apply:

Jesus wasn't bothered by the storm. In fact, He was sound asleep below deck. The disciples, however, were in a panic, convinced they were going down. To still their beating hearts, Jesus rose and spoke a few sharp words to the wind and waves: *"Be quiet! Be still."* Immediately the storm ceased.

Likely, you've been through a few storms in your life. The death of a loved one. A tough illness. A bad diagnosis. A job loss. Relationship troubles. Storms have a variety of faces. But they often throw us into a state of panic, much like the disciples found themselves in that night.

We have to remember that Jesus is in the boat with us. No matter what we're walking through, He's right there. And with just a word, He can calm the storm. *"Anxieties, be still!"*

Job situations can turn around. Sick bodies can be mended. Broken relationships can be restored. Lives can be changed in an instant if we just take our hand off the rudder and turn things over to the Lord.

Pray:

Lord, I'm so glad You're the storm calmer! You've intervened in my life so many times, I've lost count. Thank You for staying with me in the boat. I'm so grateful, Lord. Amen.

....

....

....

....

....

....

....

....

....

....

....

BLESSED ARE THOSE
WHO HAVE NOT SEEN
Read John 20:19–29

Key Verse:

*Jesus said to him, "Have you believed because
you have seen me? Blessed are those who
have not seen and yet have believed."*
JOHN 20:29 ESV

Understand:

- *Are you one of those "I won't believe it until I
  see it" types?*
- *Why do you suppose Jesus said that those who
  have not seen are more blessed?*

Apply:

Near the end of the Gospels we find a remarkable
story about one of the disciples—Thomas. The world
knows him as "Doubting Thomas," but Jesus might
disagree with that assessment.

Here's the backstory: Jesus had died on the cross
just a few days prior. Thomas saw it with his own
eyes. He knew that his friend, his mentor, his teacher
was gone. There was no disputing that cold, hard fact.

Now the other disciples were talking crazy,
saying stuff like, "We've seen Him!" Had they lost
their minds? Thomas, always the pragmatist, wanted
proof. "Unless I see in his hands the mark of the

nails, and place my finger into the mark of the nails, and place my hand into his side, I will never believe" (John 20:25 ESV).

The Lord made him wait for the proof. Eight days later, Jesus showed up, laying to rest any concerns that Thomas might have had. In an instant, as he touched the wounds in Jesus' hands and side, all doubts disappeared. The doubter became a believer.

Pray:

Lord, help me in my unbelief. There are so many times I want proof. I want to see things with my own eyes. I know that I will be more blessed if I can learn to trust You, even when I can't see. Help me, I pray. Amen.

....

....

....

....

....

....

....

....

....

....

....

PREPARE THE WAY
Read Luke 3:1–20

Key Verse:

John answered them all, "I baptize you with water.
But one who is more powerful than I will come, the straps
of whose sandals I am not worthy to untie. He will
baptize you with the Holy Spirit and fire."
LUKE 3:16 NIV

Understand:

- *It's amazing to think that God goes ahead*
  of us, getting things in order even before the
  need arises. Can you think of a time when
  you saw His hand at work like that?
- *Have you, like John the Baptist, ever gone*
  ahead of a person or situation to prepare the
  way?

Apply:

Before Jesus made His way onto the scene in ministry, His cousin, John the Baptist, carved a path, letting people know He would be coming. When Jesus arrived, advance notice had served its purpose, preparing hearts and minds for the Savior.

In life, we don't always get advance notice. Sometimes no one shows up to prepare the way. We're caught off guard when a loved one is injured in an accident or when a friendship suddenly grows cold.

We don't know what hit us when a job loss occurs or a marriage comes to an abrupt end. We crater, our nerves completely shot.

The good news is, God is never caught off guard. He knows what's coming, and He is working on our hearts to protect us. He has filled us with His Spirit to guard, comfort, and protect as we navigate through life. In other words, God won't let us down. So rest easy! Let those anxieties go. God has gone ahead of you, and all will be well.

Pray:

Thank You for going ahead of me, Lord. I know I'm safe because You've already cleared the path. I'm so grateful You've made a way through the wilderness. Amen.

....

....

....

....

....

....

....

....

....

....

LET PEACE REIGN!
Read Matthew 26:17–30

~

Key Verse:

While they were eating, Jesus took bread, and when he had given thanks, he broke it and gave it to his disciples, saying, "Take and eat; this is my body." Then he took a cup, and when he had given thanks, he gave it to them, saying, "Drink from it, all of you. This is my blood of the covenant, which is poured out for many for the forgiveness of sins."
MATTHEW 26:26–28 NIV

Understand:

- *The disciples didn't have a full understanding of what was coming, but they chose to spend as much time with Jesus as possible. Have you done that in your own life?*
- *What does the word* communion *mean to you?*

Apply:

Have you ever given thought to what must have been going through the hearts and minds of the disciples on the night they broke bread with Jesus? Did they realize that He only had a few more hours with them? Did they understand that He would actually pass away and then rise again?

Surely the disciples had the same attitude that we so often have today—they were hoping for the best but psychologically preparing for the worst.

(How many times have you done that?)

Sometimes we have an inkling that something rough is coming; other times we're caught off guard, completely unaware of what's around the bend. We do a lot of things to guard our hearts, to avoid anxiety. But God wants us to know that, even in the darkest valleys, He's still in control. He's still right there, whispering, *"Peace, be still."* So go on. . .drink from the cup. Break the bread. Commune with Him. For only in spending time with Him will true peace be found.

Pray:

Father, when I take the time to commune with You, to really spend time in Your presence, it makes such a difference in my attitude. Today I choose the peace that comes from being with You, Lord. Amen.

....

....

....

....

....

....

....

....

....

GOD WILL FIGHT FOR YOU
Read 1 Samuel 17

$\sim$

Key Verse:

David asked the men standing near him, "What will be done for the man who kills this Philistine and removes this disgrace from Israel? Who is this uncircumcised Philistine that he should defy the armies of the living God?"
1 SAMUEL 17:26 NIV

Understand:

- *Standing up to your enemies (especially the ones who loom over you) is tough! When was the last time you had to stand up to someone? How did the story end?*
- *Think of a time when God fought a battle for you.*

Apply:

If you rewound the story of David and Goliath a bit, you would see a boy on his way to the battlefield with one purpose in mind: to deliver bread and cheese. David didn't head to the army's camp to fight. He was just a delivery boy. When he heard Goliath's taunts, though, everything changed. The delivery boy morphed into a warrior. With renewed vision, he reached for five smooth stones to take down his enemy.

Maybe you've walked a mile in David's shoes.

You've somehow meandered into a situation, completely oblivious, never dreaming you'll soon be in the fight of your life. You're not even sure how you jumped from point A to point B, but there you are, standing before a giant. And you're scared. Anxious. Worried.

Isn't it wonderful to realize that God went ahead of young David and fought the battle for him? That's what He'll do for you too. Go ahead and reach for those stones. Equip yourself. But watch as the Lord of hosts fights this one for you.

Pray:

Thank You for fighting my battles, Lord! With Your help, I'll take down every giant who dares to rear his head against me! I'll praise You in advance for the victory. Amen.

....

....

....

....

....

....

....

....

....

GOOD FRUIT
Read Galatians 5:13–26

⁓

Key Verse:

But the fruit of the Spirit is love, joy, peace, forbearance, kindness, goodness, faithfulness, gentleness and self-control. Against such things there is no law.
GALATIANS 5:22–23 NIV

Understand:

- *Are there any fruits lacking in your life? How can you remedy that?*
- *When you're anxious or upset, which fruits are most beneficial to you, and why?*

Apply:

Have you ever wondered why the various fruits of the Spirit are called "fruit" in the first place? Perhaps it's because a fruit is something sweet that is produced when the vine is healthy. If you have a healthy orange tree, you'll yield a healthy crop of oranges. If your grapevine is robust, there will be juicy grapes attached.

The same is true in your life. If you stay close to your Creator, rooted and grounded in Him, your spiritual life will be healthy and robust. You'll begin to produce fruit for all to enjoy—love, joy, peace, forbearance, kindness, goodness, faithfulness, gentleness, and self-control. You won't have to summon these up; they will come as a natural result of spending time with your Savior.

So prepare yourself for a fruity future! Brace yourself for days filled with love for others, joy even in the midst of sorrow, unexplainable peace even when things are going wrong, patience with even the most annoying customer at work, and gentleness with your kiddos. God can do all this and more when you stick close to Him.

Pray:

Father, thank You for the reminder that I can see good results when I stick close to You. I want to bear fruit in my life so that I can be a good witness to others. Help me, I pray. Amen.

....

....

....

....

....

....

....

....

....

....

....

THE SHELTER OF THE MOST HIGH
Read Psalm 91

~

Key Verse:

*Whoever dwells in the shelter of the Most High
will rest in the shadow of the Almighty.*
PSALM 91:1 NIV

Understand:

- *Have you walked through a season where you
  needed God's protection and shelter? How did
  He take care of you?*
- *Have you ever had to shelter others under
  your wings?*

Apply:

If you've ever had to run for cover during a rain-storm, you know that anything will do—an awning, a car, a shopping center, even a tent. Whatever serves to hold back the rain works just fine for you.

Shelters don't just keep out the rain; they provide a psychological covering as well. When you've got something over your head, you feel safer. That's how God wants you to feel when you run to Him with your troubles. When you hide under the shadow of His wings (as a baby chick would hide under its mother's wings), He's got you covered. He's like a papa bear, daring anyone to mess with His cub.

Here's an interesting fact: God wants to keep

you covered at all times. But let's face it. . .we have a way of tucking ourselves under other, counterfeit shelters. Maybe it's time to do an assessment, to make sure you've got the right covering. Whatever you're facing, God wants to protect you as you go through it.

Pray:

Thank You for the reminder that You're my Protector, Lord! I'll do my best not to run to the counterfeit shelters when I've got the real deal. Amen.

....

....

....

....

....

....

....

....

....

....

....

....

HE ANSWERED ME
Read Genesis 21:1–21

Key Verse:

Now the LORD was gracious to Sarah as he had said, and the LORD did for Sarah what he had promised. Sarah became pregnant and bore a son to Abraham in his old age, at the very time God had promised him.
GENESIS 21:1–2 NIV

Understand:

- *During anxious seasons, it's easy to give up. Have you ever had to persevere like Abraham and Sarah? What was the outcome of your perseverance?*
- *God moved in a miraculous way in Sarah's life. Have you ever experienced a miracle in your own life?*

Apply:

Abraham and Sarah were elderly when their son, Isaac, was born. No wonder Sarah laughed when she learned she was having a child. Not many women in their golden years give birth to babies!

Isaac was the long-awaited promise, the child they'd always longed for. His arrival was the culmination of many years of hoping, praying, and believing despite the odds.

Maybe you've been waiting a long time for

something—a spouse, a child, a new job, a home. You've pleaded with God, and it all seems to be in vain. You're nearly ready to give up. Circumstances have almost convinced you it's never going to happen.

Today, let your faith be invigorated again. Read through Abraham and Sarah's story and allow your heart to dream once more. God is a dream giver and a dream fulfiller. Allow Him to see this miracle all the way through.

Pray:

Father, thank You for the reminder that the dreams You've laid on my heart are God breathed and will be God fulfilled. I remove my hands and choose to trust You today, Lord. Amen.

....

....

....

....

....

....

....

....

....

....

A TREK THROUGH THE DESERT
Read Joshua 1

⁓

Key Verse:

"Moses my servant is dead. Now then, you and all these people, get ready to cross the Jordan River into the land I am about to give to them—to the Israelites. I will give you every place where you set your foot, as I promised Moses."
JOSHUA 1:2–3 NIV

Understand:

- *We don't always reach the promised land in a hurry. Think of a time when you had to wait on your miracle.*
- *What have you learned as you've trekked through the desert?*

Apply:

The Israelites wandered in the desert for forty long years. A journey that should have taken them weeks took far longer. It was riddled with complications, rebellion, frustration, and so on.

Maybe you feel a bit like you're trekking through the desert right now. Your promised land isn't far off. You've got it in your sights. But there are times when you wonder if you'll ever pass over the river and actually enter. The process just seems too hard, the anxieties too great.

Maybe you're a couple of college courses away

from your degree, but nothing is going right. Or perhaps your income is just a bit too low to get that house you're dreaming of. Maybe you're inches away from getting that job promotion you deserve and wondering if it will ever come through. You're right at the brink of your miracle, but it seems to be eluding you.

Don't give up! You will cross over the Jordan in God's time. And when you do, you can celebrate in style. Until then, don't continue to trek through the heat and sand. Stop and bask in God's promise. He will see you through.

Pray:

Lord, sometimes I feel like I won't make it to the promised land. I'm tempted to give up. Thank You for the reminder that You're with me, even in the desert. Increase my faith today, I pray. Amen.

....

....

....

....

....

....

....

....

BE THE ANSWER (GIDEON)
Read Judges 7

~

Key Verse:

During that night the LORD said to Gideon,
"Get up, go down against the camp, because I am
going to give it into your hands."
JUDGES 7:9 NIV

Understand:

- *Surely there were times when Gideon felt like giving up. What about you? Have you ever been tempted to quit?*
- *Gideon's army grew smaller and smaller until the core group emerged. The same is likely true in your life. Who's in your core group?*

Apply:

Gideon did as God instructed. He minimized his army. In the natural this doesn't make a bit of sense. When you're headed into battle, you want to come at your enemy with all you've got. But Gideon whittled down his troops until he had only three hundred men. No doubt he was secretly worried about whether they could pull this one off!

It's interesting to note that God trimmed back the size of Israel's army so that they wouldn't boast later on that they had won the battle in their own strength. There are probably times in all our lives when we take credit for things we've worked hard at—weight loss, a job promotion, good grades, and so on. Sure, we play a role in those things (a big role), but the victory is God's to claim.

Is God asking you to trim back your army today? Maybe you've been overthinking something. Maybe it's consuming you. Trim back. . .and trust God. He's got this.

Pray:

Lord, may I be like Gideon, willing to trust You, even when You ask me to do things that make no sense. Today I choose to trim back areas of my life that have consumed me. I give them to You, Lord. Amen.

....

....

....

....

....

....

....

....

....

....

A SOUND MIND
Read Luke 4:1–13

⌒

Key Verse:

*When the devil had ended every temptation,
he departed from him until an opportune time.*
LUKE 4:13 ESV

Understand:

- *Think of a time when the enemy reared his
  head against you. Did you fall for his lies?*
- *When you're tempted to give in to the enemy's
  tactics, what can you do to turn things
  around?*

Apply:

If you read the opening lines of this story, you'll learn
a lot: Jesus was full of the Holy Spirit and led by the
Holy Spirit into the wilderness. When you submit
yourself to the Spirit of God, when you say, "I'll let
You be the one to lead and guide me," then you're
always in a safe place.

Like Jesus, we will go through seasons of temptation. The enemy will do everything in his power to
veer us off in the wrong direction. We might even
wonder why or how we got to a place of confusion.

But when we're full of the Spirit of God, when
we're completely and wholly submitted to the process of learning all we can learn, we have to trust that

God is still in control, even when we're in the middle of the wilderness.

Where are you today? Feeling a little lost? Wondering how you got there? Instead of questioning the Lord or letting anxieties get the best of you, ask the Spirit of God to fill you to the top. He will guide you exactly where you need to go.

Pray:

I know that the safest place to be, Lord, is where Your Spirit guides me. Fill me today, I pray, and lead me where You will. I will gladly follow. Amen.

....

....

....

....

....

....

....

....

....

....

....

A HOLY INTERRUPTION
Read Luke 2:8–21

⌒

Key Verse:

"Glory to God in the highest, and on earth peace among those with whom he is pleased!"
LUKE 2:14 ESV

Understand:

- *The shepherds were just minding their own business when God interrupted their lives in an amazing way. Think of a time when that happened to you.*
- *Why do you suppose God chose lowly shepherds instead of, say, well-to-do villagers?*

Apply:

Picture this: You've just fallen asleep. You're somewhere between that lovely twilight sleep and deeper REM sleep. All cares of the world are long forgotten. All anxieties erased. Tomorrow's cares can take care of themselves.

The sheep on the hillside? They're snoozing too. Right now, it's just you and your dreams.

Then, from out of nowhere, an angelic choir lights the night with a radiant glow and music from on high. For a moment you wonder if you're dreaming. Then, just as quickly, you realize you're awake.

You rub your eyes and stare. This can't be real, can it?

This is exactly what happened to the shepherds on the night Jesus was born. One minute they were sound asleep, the next they were on the road to Bethlehem to worship the babe.

Life can change in an instant with one holy interruption. One minute you're snoozing, the next you're headed off on a journey you didn't even know you were going to take. That's why you've got to be prepared, in season and out. The shepherds? They were ready to jump and run.

What about you? If God interrupts your life, will you be ready?

Pray:

Lord, I want to be ready for holy interruptions. I can't wait to see where You're taking me next, Father! Amen.

....

....

....

....

....

....

....

....

....

USABLE, IN SPITE OF
Read 1 Timothy 4

$\frown$

Key Verse:

Don't let anyone look down on you because you are young, but set an example for the believers in speech, in conduct, in love, in faith and in purity.
1 TIMOTHY 4:12 NIV

Understand:

- *Have you ever felt unqualified for a task? How did you manage to overcome those feelings of inadequacy?*
- *Think of the names of a few people who have encouraged you along the way and who have said, "You've got this!"*

Apply:

Timothy was relatively young (probably in his twenties) when he took on the role of evangelist. Some would argue that he hadn't done his time, that he didn't have enough notches on his belt, that he needed more life experience when the call of God propelled him into ministry.

Maybe you can relate. Maybe God called you at a young age or when you didn't feel psychologically ready. Maybe inadequacies or anxieties arose. Maybe folks nearby whispered, "Why did she get picked? I'm a better candidate."

It's hard to know how and why God chooses the ones He does, but you can trust in the choosing. If the Lord calls, He will equip. It's that simple. So rest easy! The task ahead might seem daunting. You might think you don't have the goods. Today God wants you to know that He does. He's got all you need and more.

Pray:

Lord, I rarely feel completely adequate or prepared for the tasks You put in front of me. Many times, I think You've called the wrong person. But today I choose to submit to the task. If You've called me, Lord, I know You will equip me. I'm trusting in that promise today. Amen.

....

....

....

....

....

....

....

....

....

....

....

HOPE IN THE PIT
Read Genesis 37

~

Key Verse:

They said to one another, "Here comes this dreamer. Come now, let us kill him and throw him into one of the pits. Then we will say that a fierce animal has devoured him, and we will see what will become of his dreams."
GENESIS 37:19–20 ESV

Understand:

- *Joseph was thrown into the pit by his own brothers. Have you ever been betrayed by someone you trusted? How did you overcome?*
- *Even in the pit, Joseph never gave up. Maybe you've walked a mile in Joseph's shoes. How do you keep your head up, even when circumstances seem to be against you?*

Apply:

Some would argue that young Joseph had it coming. All that bragging about being the favored child didn't exactly put him in good standing with his brothers, after all. Those dreams of his were a source of contention among the siblings.

But imagine finding yourself at the bottom of a pit, bruised, dirty, and hurting, while those you thought you could trust jeered at you from above. The feelings of betrayal must have been overwhelming.

Perhaps Joseph even wondered if those dreams of his had been from God or were the result of something bad he'd eaten.

Maybe you've been there. You've faced betrayal from someone you trusted—a spouse, a parent, a child, a sibling, a friend. You're staring up, up, up from the bottom of a pit, your heart broken into a thousand pieces as your dreams seemingly come to an end.

Just remember, Joseph's story didn't end in the pit. God redeemed the situation and turned everything around. He'll do the very same for you. So don't give up. The Lord has big plans for you, and they're just around the corner.

Pray:

Father, I feel so betrayed. Those who claimed to care about me turned their backs on me when I least suspected. Like Joseph, I feel as if I'm in a pit. Rescue me, I pray. Give me hope, comfort, and deliverance. Amen.

....

....

....

....

....

....

....

LEAD ME TO THE ROCK
Read Psalm 61

Key Verse:

From the end of the earth I call to you when my heart is faint. Lead me to the rock that is higher than I.
PSALM 61:2 ESV

Understand:

- *When we are at our weakest, God proves His strength. Think of a time when He did this for you.*
- *Sometimes we run toward God. Other times we crawl, barely able to gather the strength. Think of a time when you barely made it to the Rock.*

Apply:

The Bible often refers to Jesus as the Rock. Maybe you've read the story of the wise man who built his house upon the rock. When you build your life—your family, your business, your hopes, your dreams, your hobbies—on Jesus, you will succeed.

Maybe you've been in shifting-sand mode of late. Maybe your business is crumbling or your marriage is in trouble. Maybe you've wandered out from under God's covering, seeking other pleasures. It's not too late to turn around and head back to the Rock. Jesus is right there, waiting.

If your heart is faint today, if you're tired of doing things your way, then run to Jesus. His ways are higher. His thoughts are higher. His plan to redeem you is higher. And remember, when you are at your very weakest, God longs to show you His strength.

So what's holding you back? Run to the Rock.

Pray:

Lord, there have been so many times when I've felt weak, unable to keep going. If not for You, my Rock, I would surely have given up by now. Thank You for holding steady, even when everything else in my life feels like shifting sand. I'm so grateful, Lord. Amen.

....

....

....

....

....

....

....

....

....

....

....

CONSOLATION
Read Jeremiah 31

Key Verse:

The LORD appeared to us in the past, saying: "I have loved you with an everlasting love; I have drawn you with unfailing kindness. I will build you up again, and you, Virgin Israel, will be rebuilt. Again you will take up your timbrels and go out to dance with the joyful."
JEREMIAH 31:3–4 NIV

Understand:

- *Have you ever walked through a season where you felt inconsolable? How did you get through it?*
- *How has God used you to console a friend or loved one?*

Apply:

Jeremiah is known as the weeping prophet. Maybe you can relate to that description. Perhaps you're the sort of person who feels things deeply, who has a hard time hiding your emotions.

The truth is, Jeremiah had a lot to weep over. He faced persecution from those who disagreed with him, conflicts with false prophets, and untold plots against him.

Perhaps you've felt like that at times, like the whole world is conspiring against you. Maybe you've adopted a "What's the point?" attitude. Things are just too hard. The pressure is too great. Your anxieties have gotten the best of you.

If so, then look up! Your redemption is drawing near. Jeremiah's story ended triumphantly, with God's assurance that He would turn mourning into dancing. He will do the same in your life. No matter what you're going through right now, redemption is coming. God will rebuild, restore, and renew your life and give you purpose once more.

Pray:

Thank You for restoring my life, Lord. I don't want to live in defeat. I want to lift my eyes, dry my tears, and give every anxiety to You. I know I can trust You, Father. Amen.

....

....

....

....

....

....

....

....

....

CAST THOSE CARES
Read John 21:1–14

~

Key Verse:

He said, "Throw your net on the right side of the boat and you will find some." When they did, they were unable to haul the net in because of the large number of fish.
JOHN 21:6 NIV

Understand:

- *Have you ever held on to your cares unnecessarily? When God asks you to toss them overboard, go for it!*
- *Can you think of a time when God told you to "fish" on the other side of the boat? He's in the provision business and wants to bless you.*

Apply:

When Jesus instructed the disciples to cast their nets on the opposite side of the boat, He was giving them several opportunities at once: to obey, to trust, and to prosper. Maybe He's given you similar challenges at times. He was also giving them the option of doing things His way instead of their own.

It's not always easy to do things God's way, but when you do, your burdens are lifted. As you cast that net on His side of the boat, you're releasing the cares and anxieties that came with trying to do things your own way.

What is God asking you to trust Him with today? Can you cast your net on His side of the boat, let go of your worries, and trust Him to give you a large haul? Get ready to obey, and you will see amazing results!

Pray:

Lord, today I choose to obey You—to toss my net on Your side of the boat, that I might see a haul. I release my cares, my anxieties, and my need to control, and I choose to trust You instead. Praise You, Father! Amen.

....

....

....

....

....

....

....

....

....

....

....

....

THE WALLS COME TUMBLING DOWN

Read Joshua 6

⌒

Key Verse:

*When the trumpets sounded, the army shouted,
and at the sound of the trumpet, when the men gave
a loud shout, the wall collapsed; so everyone
charged straight in, and they took the city.*
JOSHUA 6:20 NIV

Understand:

- *Are there any walls in your life right now,
  separating you from God or others?*
- *How is God nudging you to get rid of barriers
  in your life?*

Apply:

The walls of Jericho came tumbling down when Joshua took the time to follow God's plan. He could have tried to knock the wall down in his own strength, but that would have taken ages (and the noise would have alerted the enemy). God had a plan to take those walls down instantaneously!

Maybe you can relate to Joshua's story. Maybe there are walls in your life that need to come down—between you and your spouse, between friends or coworkers, perhaps even between you and God. Instead of chipping away at them, ask God to bring those walls down in a flash. Take authority over the situation. March around those walls (spiritually speaking) and let out a shout; then watch as God miraculously takes over.

Walls are no hindrance for God. And, as you watch them tumble, they won't be a hindrance for you either.

Pray:

I love the story of Joshua, Lord! It's so exciting to watch
You move so quickly. I ask You to do that in my life
as well. I submit my walls to You, Father.
Knock them down, I pray. Amen.

....

....

....

....

....

....

....

....

....

....

....

BUILD A WHAT?
Read Genesis 6:9–7:24

~

Key Verse:

*On that very day Noah and his sons, Shem, Ham and
Japheth, together with his wife and the wives of his three
sons, entered the ark. They had with them every wild animal
according to its kind, all livestock according to their kinds,
every creature that moves along the ground according
to its kind and every bird according to its
kind, everything with wings.*
GENESIS 7:13–14 NIV

Understand:

- *Noah was a man of extreme faith. He and his
  sons surely faced ridicule and gossip. Have you
  ever been in a situation where God asked you
  to do something that made no sense (to you or
  to others)?*
- *Has society changed much since Noah's day?*

Apply:

Think about this for a moment: before Noah and
the ark, no one had ever seen rain. And no one had
ever seen a boat either. So, when God spoke to Noah
and gave him instructions to build, can you imagine
Noah's confusion? Build a what? Out of what? For
what?

Maybe you've felt confused at God's instructions

in your life at times. Maybe He's spoken something to your heart that makes no sense at all. You wanted to stare at heaven and say, "I don't get it, Lord. I don't understand."

The good news is, we don't have to understand. We just have to move in faith when God calls us to. And even when things make no sense to us whatsoever, we can trust that the Lord has big plans for us, if we will just follow His lead. There are rainbows ahead if we will just move forward with our hand in His.

Pray:

I choose to follow You, Lord, even when I don't fully understand Your instructions. If You could lead Noah and his family to safety, then I know You've got my best interest at heart. I trust You, Father. Amen.

....

....

....

....

....

....

....

....

....

FAITH TO BELIEVE (ABRAM)
Read Genesis 15

⌒

Key Verse:

*Abram believed the LORD, and he credited
it to him as righteousness.*
GENESIS 15:6 NIV

Understand:

- *Think of a time when your situation called
  for the same extreme sort of faith that Abram
  had to muster.*
- *Believing for the impossible seems, well,
  impossible at times. How has God restored
  your faith during difficult seasons?*

Apply:

God gave Abram a promise that he would be the
father of many nations. This announcement came
when Abram had no children at all. Years passed.
His wife did not give birth. But he never forgot the
promise from the Lord. While circumstantial evi-
dence mounted against him, Abram began to wonder if, perhaps, he had misunderstood God's plan.

Maybe you've been there. Like Abram, you've
heard from the Lord. He's made you a promise.
You'll have a career. A spouse. A child. A home.
You've waited. . .then waited some more. You're now
at the "Will it ever happen?" point.

It sounds cliché to say, "Just have faith," but that's the answer. If you keep your faith high and your doubts low, you'll suffer less while you're waiting. Don't give up on what you know the Lord has promised. He's not a promise breaker.

Pray:

Thank You for fulfilling Your promises, Lord. I know I can trust You. While I'm waiting—even when the storms come, Lord—I won't give up. I'll continue to have faith. Amen.

....

....

....

....

....

....

....

....

....

....

....

....

....

PERSISTENCE PAYS OFF
Read 1 Samuel 1:1–20

⌒

Key Verse:

*So in the course of time Hannah became pregnant
and gave birth to a son. She named him Samuel,
saying, "Because I asked the LORD for him."*
1 SAMUEL 1:20 NIV

Understand:

- *Hannah pleaded with God for quite some
  time before she conceived Samuel. Have you
  ever had to have faith for a prolonged time?*
- *What do you do when you're desperate for a
  miracle but God is silent?*

Apply:

Poor Hannah. She was loved by God and by her
husband, who adored her, but her womb had been
closed. Her heart broke over the child she so des-
perately wanted. And it didn't help matters that her
archrival spent much of her time provoking Hannah
in order to cause jealousy.

Hannah pleaded her case before the Lord, and
God heard her cries. He gave her a son, Samuel, and
the course of history was changed because of the role
he played in selecting King David.

Have you ever found yourself in Hannah's shoes?
You're holding out for a miracle, but someone around

you is tormenting you? Ridiculing? Making fun of your dream?

Don't give up, even when anxiety threatens to rear its head. Don't let jealousy enter the picture. Don't get anxious. Keep your heart pure as you wait, and watch what God is about to do. Perhaps, when your dream is fulfilled, it will change the course of history as well.

Pray:

Lord, I give my hopes, wishes, and dreams to You. I lay down anxieties and say, "In Your time, Father!" I close my ears to the naysayers and keep my focus on You while I'm waiting, Lord. Amen.

....

....

....

....

....

....

....

....

....

....

....

THE BLIND WILL SEE
Read John 9

Key Verse:

Therefore the Pharisees also asked him how he had received his sight. "He put mud on my eyes," the man replied, "and I washed, and now I see."
JOHN 9:15 NIV

Understand:

- *Jesus used an unconventional method to heal the blind man. Has He ever moved unconventionally in your life?*
- *The Pharisees questioned the man intensely. Have people ever quizzed you after a miraculous season?*

Apply:

As Jesus journeyed from place to place, He was pulled aside to pray for a variety of people. One of them, a blind man, had an interesting encounter with the Savior. Jesus used a rather unconventional method to heal the man (something he would never forget). Afterward, the Pharisees wouldn't leave this poor guy alone. They pelted him with questions about Jesus and did all they could to cast doubt on the situation.

Have you ever been in a situation where the doubters began to interject their questions and thoughts? You couldn't even celebrate your miracle before they started picking away at it, questioning everything.

Life is filled with doubters, many of whom refuse to see what's in front of them. Today, as you continue to pray for your miracle, pray for the people who walk in blindness, who refuse to see God's goodness. Perhaps your prayers will play a role in opening their eyes!

Pray:

I pray for all eyes to be opened today, Lord—my own, and all of those around me who might doubt Your goodness. Let every shackle fall, I pray. Amen.

....

....

....

....

....

....

....

....

....

....

....

FOR SUCH A TIME AS THIS
Read Esther 4

Key Verse:

"For if you remain silent at this time, relief and deliverance for the Jews will arise from another place, but you and your father's family will perish. And who knows but that you have come to your royal position for such a time as this?"
ESTHER 4:14 NIV

Understand:

- *Esther was born at a particular time, in a particular place, for a particular people. Have you ever considered the fact that God chose the era and location of your birth for a reason?*
- *God showed Esther great favor. Have you ever walked through a season of favor like that?*

Apply:

When Esther was a little girl, it probably never occurred to her that one day she would play a pivotal role in saving her people. Surely she considered herself ordinary. Typical.

Maybe you're the same. You look at your life and you think, *Who am I to do anything extraordinary?* You wonder if God can use you to accomplish anything in the lives of others.

Here's the truth: You are created in the image of

God and filled with the Spirit of God. Even on your worst day, when you're riddled with anxiety, the Lord can use you. And that's what He longs to do. There are people in your circle who need you. They need your humor, your expertise, your love. They need your reassurance that they matter. You can—and will—make a difference in the lives of many, many people, if you just believe.

So brush off those concerns. Square your shoulders. Begin to see yourself as usable to the kingdom of God. Who knows but that you were born for such a time as this?

Pray:

Thank You for the reminder that I was born to make a difference in my world, Lord. Today I choose to believe that I was born for this very time and this very place. Amen.

....

....

....

....

....

....

....

....

....

WHO ARE THE *THEYS*?
Read Luke 5:17–26

⌒

Key Verse:

Some men took a man who was not able to move his body to Jesus. He was carried on a bed. They looked for a way to take the man into the house where Jesus was. But they could not find a way to take him in because of so many people. They made a hole in the roof over where Jesus stood. Then they let the bed with the sick man on it down before Jesus.
LUKE 5:18–19 NLV

Understand:

- *What amazing friends, to carry their friend all the way to the Healer! Do you have any friends like that?*
- *How can you be a better friend to someone who struggles with a chronic health issue?*

Apply:

They brought their friend to Jesus. *They* lowered him through the room. *They* went out of their way to make sure the one in need had a chance to be seen, noticed.

This story is filled with hints that the one in need had a solid group of friends who cared. Hopefully, you've got a similar group. Who are the *theys* in your life? Who would move heaven and earth on your behalf?

The truth is, we were never meant to do life alone. We all need *theys*. If you're in a lonely season, if the *theys* have vanished, then make up your mind to be a *they* to others. Draw close to one in need—a shut-in, a cancer patient, the woman whose husband left her alone to raise her children without him. Become part of the circle of caring, loving people; then watch as God replenishes your own circle of friends.

Pray:

I needed this reminder, Lord, that I was never meant to do life alone. Encircle me with people who care, I pray, and help me draw close to others, that I might be a they as well. Amen.

....

....

....

....

....

....

....

....

....

....

....

IN SPITE OF
Read Job 1

◠

Key Verse:

In all this Job did not sin or blame God.
JOB 1:22 NLV

Understand:

- *Have you ever wanted to point the finger at God, to blame Him for the bad things happening in your life?*
- *Where is God when things are falling apart?*

Apply:

In spite of everything, Job did not sin or blame God. Let those words sink in for a moment. In spite of pain. Sickness. Death. Loss. Destruction.

Us? We're so quick to blame. When a meal isn't right, we blame the cook or waitress. When our team doesn't win, we blame the umpire or referee. When we show up late for an event, we're loaded with excuses for how others slowed us down.

Pointing the finger is a natural defense, but maybe it's time to adopt Job's attitude. Even when he lost everything, he didn't point the finger at God. He could have. (Let's face it, most of us would.) He could have pointed to heaven and shouted, "Why are You doing this to me? What did I ever do to You?"

The truth is, even in the hardest of times, God

wants us to keep our eyes fixed on Him and our hope elevated. So toss those anxieties out the window. Stop blaming. Keep your eyes on the One who plans to deliver you; then watch as He works all things together for your good.

Pray:

I needed that reminder today, Lord! I'm so quick to point the finger. Today I choose to adopt Job's stance and remind myself that, in spite of everything, You are still good. Amen.

....

....

....

....

....

....

....

....

....

....

....

....

A VICTORY HYMN
Read Judges 4–5

~

Key Verse:

Now Deborah, a prophetess, the wife of Lappidoth, was judging Israel at that time. She used to sit under the palm of Deborah between Ramah and Bethel in the hill country of Ephraim, and the people of Israel came up to her for judgment.
JUDGES 4:4–5 ESV

Understand:

- *This is one of the few times that a female is listed as a prophetess of God. What do you think of God using women in a role such as this?*
- *Why do you suppose Judges 5 recounts the same story as Judges 4, only in poetic form?*

Apply:

Deborah was a prophetess of God and the only female judge ever mentioned in the Bible. (Talk about being a standout!) She sat under a palm tree between Ramah and Bethel in the hill country, where people would come to her for judgment.

Deborah had a strong prophetic gifting. She shared with Barak (a military commander of that time) that God had commanded him to attack Jabin, the king of Canaan, as well as Sisera, Jabin's military commander.

Stop and picture this for a moment. A woman, telling a man to attack and kill another man? In biblical times, this was almost unheard of.

Many would say that it should still be unheard of, that women are to be seen and not heard in church. There are a couple of scriptures that seem to lean in that direction. Taken in context (the culture of that day being quite different from today), some would argue that women have a perfect right to minister. Regardless of what you believe on that score, Deborah certainly led the way for godly women.

Pray:

Thank You for the reminder that women are usable, Lord! You've never excluded women from Your plan, and I'm so grateful. Amen.

....

....

....

....

....

....

....

....

....

USHERED IN!
Read John 4:1–26

$\frown$

Key Verse:

The Samaritan woman said to him, "You are a Jew and I am a Samaritan woman. How can you ask me for a drink?" (For Jews do not associate with Samaritans.)
JOHN 4:9 NIV

Understand:

- *Jesus spoke with such compassion and love to the woman at the well. Do you ever marvel at His ability to speak with such love to you, even when you're caught in sin?*
- *What was the living water that Jesus spoke of in this chapter?*

Apply:

The woman at the well didn't set off to have a one-on-one encounter with the Savior of the world. She was just going about her daily routine, gathering water at the well. When the stranger struck up a conversation with her, she couldn't help but be drawn in. He was, after all, a Jew. She was a Samaritan, and an outcast at that. The idea that He would speak to her at all was mesmerizing.

And all those things He said! He seemed to know everything about her. To top it off, He spoke with such compassion, such love, that she found herself completely at ease.

Have you ever felt like that woman—outcast, set apart from the crowd? Have you wondered if Jesus would welcome you into a conversation? Maybe you've judged yourself harshly and convinced yourself that you don't fit in with other Christians.

Think again. God welcomes all. If Jesus took the time to speak with such love and affection to this woman, then surely He will usher you into His presence as well.

Pray:

Father, I feel like I don't fit in at times. Thank You for including me, for putting me at ease and welcoming me in that loving, tender way. I'm so grateful, Lord. Amen.

....

....

....

....

....

....

....

....

....

....

DON'T SELL OUT
Read Genesis 25:19–34

Key Verse:

But Jacob said, "Swear to me first." So he swore an oath to him, selling his birthright to Jacob.
GENESIS 25:33 NIV

Understand:

- *Think of a time when you "sold out." Did you have regrets? How did the Lord redeem the situation?*
- *Have you ever experienced sibling rivalry? Did things get rough?*

Apply:

You've likely heard of people making bad deals, but this is the worst! Esau, in a fit of hunger, sold his birthright to his brother. . .for a bowl of stew. Really? Talk about an impulsive decision. And imagine the regrets. How would you like to wake up the following morning and have to face the fact that you'd lost everything because of a temporary problem?

Maybe you can relate. Maybe you've cut a deal with someone to satisfy a temporary itch only to regret it later. Cheating on a test. Lying on a tax return. Breaking a confidence. Breaking a marriage vow to spend a few fleeting moments with someone younger, more tempting.

These things seem to satisfy an itch, but they cause deep, long-lasting regrets later.

Don't sell out. If you take anything away from Jacob and Esau's story, let it be this: it's not worth it. Don't give up everything for temporary satisfaction. The regrets will wreck you.

Pray:

Father, for the many times I've sold out, I repent.
Please forgive me and straighten out my thinking.
I don't want to sell myself or You short, Lord.
May all my deals be good deals from now on. Amen.

....

....

....

....

....

....

....

....

....

....

....

POWER AND AUTHORITY
Read Luke 9:1–17

⌒

Key Verse:

When Jesus had called the Twelve together, he gave them power and authority to drive out all demons and to cure diseases, and he sent them out to proclaim the kingdom of God and to heal the sick.
LUKE 9:1–2 NIV

Understand:

- *God has given you authority, just as He gave the disciples. What's the most amazing thing you've witnessed as you've used this authority?*
- *Have you ever prayed for a sick person and watched that person be healed?*

Apply:

Can you even imagine what the disciples must have been thinking as Jesus spoke words of power and authority over them? Picture yourself in their shoes, with the King of the universe looking you in the eye and saying, *"I give you all power and authority to perform miracles, to drive out demons, to cure diseases, and to proclaim the Gospel message!"*

Wow! That will certainly push your anxieties and fears aside, won't it?

Here's the truth: Jesus has spoken those very

same words over you. You have that same authority to speak life into situations, to pray over impossible circumstances, and to witness miracles. You have the power to preach the Gospel, to share the love of Jesus with the unsaved, and to help those who are caught up in addiction.

Begin to claim that authority. Walk it out. Speak with faith and confidence as you pray in Jesus' name. Then, brace yourself! Miracles are surely on their way.

Pray:

I'm so grateful for Your authority, Jesus! When I speak in Your name, my words carry a lot of weight. Like the disciples, I will make a difference in my world. Thank You, Lord. Amen.

....

....

....

....

....

....

....

....

....

....

....

PRAISE YOUR WAY THROUGH
Read 2 Chronicles 20:1–30

⌒

Key Verse:

After consulting the people, Jehoshaphat appointed men to sing to the LORD and to praise him for the splendor of his holiness as they went out at the head of the army, saying: "Give thanks to the LORD, for his love endures forever."
2 CHRONICLES 20:21 NIV

Understand:

- *Just as the Levites went ahead of the army in praise, God wants praise to lead the way in your life too. What problem are you facing today? Lift a song of praise!*
- *What's the hardest situation you ever walked through? How did praise play a role in getting you through?*

Apply:

When Jehoshaphat faced his opposition, he surely felt both anxious and overwhelmed. His strategy for success? Send the Levites (singers) to the front lines, ahead of the warriors. Jehoshaphat literally praised his way into the battle, a song of praise leading the way. Might sound like a funny way to win a battle, but that's exactly what happened. The opposition fell, the Israelites won, and God got the victory!

The same strategy will work in your life. When

you're facing an enemy of any sort, when the battle around you rages on, reach for your strongest weapon first—praise. If you start out with a song of praise on your lips, it will do two things: boost your courage and confound your enemy.

What opposition are you facing today? Look it squarely in the eye with a song of praise in your heart; then watch God give you the victory over that situation.

Pray:

Lord, I'm so glad I can praise my way through my battles. I know I can always stand victorious in the end if I lead the way with praise. You'll give me the victory, Father! Amen.

....

....

....

....

....

....

....

....

....

....

BLINDED BY THE LIGHT
Read Acts 9:1-9

⌒

Key Verse:

As he journeyed he came near Damascus, and suddenly a light shone around him from heaven. Then he fell to the ground, and heard a voice saying to him, "Saul, Saul, why are you persecuting Me?"
ACTS 9:3–4 NKJV

Understand:

- *Saul was moving in one direction in his life and then suddenly. . .bam! God stopped him in his tracks and turned his story around. Have you ever had an abrupt change like that?*
- *Have you known any Sauls, people whose lives were radically transformed?*

Apply:

So many Bible stories (like this one) begin with a person having an ordinary day, doing an ordinary thing. Saul was just walking down the road, something he'd done hundreds of times before. Then, before he knew what hit him, a bright light blinded him and put a halt to his journey.

Saul's loss of vision was just the first of many things that would happen. God spoke very clearly to him and completely shifted his life journey. No longer would he be Saul the persecutor. He would be Paul, the evangelist who would change the course of history and whose name would be known thousands of years later.

Sometimes we have to be blinded in order to see. Maybe you've been there. God had to distract you with a supernatural experience to get your attention. Regardless of His tactic, the Lord has one goal in mind—to put you on the road that will lead to heaven.

Pray:

Lord, I don't want You to have to intervene in my life in a supernatural way to get my attention. May I be focused on You and moving in the direction You want me to go. Today I recommit my life to You, Jesus. May I only ever follow You. Amen.

....

....

....

....

....

....

....

....

WHEN ALL GOES WELL
Read Matthew 21:1–11

⁓

Key Verse:

Most of the crowd spread their cloaks on the road, and others cut branches from the trees and spread them on the road. And the crowds that went before him and that followed him were shouting, "Hosanna to the Son of David! Blessed is he who comes in the name of the Lord! Hosanna in the highest!"
MATTHEW 21:8–9 ESV

Understand:

- *It's ironic to think that Jesus was ushered into Jerusalem with such fanfare, only to be crucified shortly thereafter. What do you think He went through emotionally?*
- *Have you ever walked through a season of favor that was quickly followed by a season of loss?*

Apply:

What an amazing day this must have been! Jesus entered Jerusalem, riding on a colt, to a welcoming crowd—one filled with onlookers and fans who cried out, "Hosanna to the Son of David! Blessed is he who comes in the name of the Lord!" They spoke blessings over Him, words of affirmation and adoration.

What different words they shouted a week later,

as Jesus carried the cross to Golgotha. On that day onlookers jeered, spit on Him, and ridiculed Him.

A lot can change in a week.

Maybe you know what it feels like to be favored one moment then disregarded and cast aside the next. Maybe your husband left you for another woman. Maybe your child stopped speaking to you. Maybe you were overlooked by your boss, passed over for a promotion.

When all goes well, it's easy to shout words of praise. But when things are crumbling around you, depression and anxiety can set in. Today God wants you to know that He's got your back, no matter what you're going through. Good or bad, happy or sad, He will get you through this.

Pray:

I needed that reminder, Lord! I don't want to celebrate only when things are going my way. I want to be found faithful, even during the hard seasons. May I never forget that You won't let me go, Father. Amen.

....

....

....

....

....

....

....

GET IN THE RIVER
Read Ezekiel 47:1–12

⌒

Key Verse:

As the man went eastward with a measuring line in his hand, he measured off a thousand cubits and then led me through water that was ankle-deep. He measured off another thousand cubits and led me through water that was knee-deep. He measured off another thousand and led me through water that was up to the waist.
EZEKIEL 47:3–4 NIV

Understand:

- *As you analyze your walk with God, would you say that you are ankle deep, knee deep, or waist deep?*
- *Is there anything about the word* surrender *that frightens you?*

Apply:

If you've ever gone swimming in the ocean, then the story of Ezekiel is probably easy for you to picture. You start off on the shore, toes pressed into the sand. Then, you take those first few steps toward the water. It soon covers the tops of your feet. A few more steps and it's up to your shins. Then your knees. Then your hips. Then, eventually, you're waist deep.

It doesn't take much effort to go deeper in the ocean. The same is true when it comes to your walk with God. He wants to take you much deeper than you are now, to a place of sweet communion and fellowship with Him.

What's holding you back today? Is there a reason you feel safer only wading in up to your ankles? Are you afraid of the commitment? Afraid God will ask you to give up something you love? The truth is, God has your best interest at heart. As you go deeper and deeper with Him, you will discover that His love washes over you, removing any worries and concerns you might have had. All He really wants is your heart—your whole heart.

Pray:

I want to go deeper with You, Lord. Take me well beyond where I am now—not ankle deep or even knee deep. I want to find myself immersed in Your Spirit, Lord, completely overwhelmed by Your presence. My heart is Yours, Lord. Amen.

....

....

....

....

....

....

....

....

WISE MEN SEEK HIM
Read Matthew 2:1–12

⌒

Key Verse:

Then Herod called the Magi secretly and found out from them the exact time the star had appeared. He sent them to Bethlehem and said, "Go and search carefully for the child. As soon as you find him, report to me, so that I too may go and worship him."
MATTHEW 2:7–8 NIV

Understand:

- *Have you ever given thought to the gifts that the magi brought the baby Jesus? Which one intrigues you most?*
- *Perhaps you've heard the phrase "Wise men still seek Him." What does this mean to you?*

Apply:

Isn't it fascinating that God chose to include magi (wise men) in the story of the Savior's birth? The concept of highly educated people seeking out the baby in the manger intrigues us all. Perhaps we're most curious about who these men were and why they were so interested in the Messiah's birth.

How wonderful to know that wise men (and women) still seek Him!

Think back to the first time you ever heard about Jesus. The story intrigued you. You stopped everything to check it out. If what you were learning was true, it would change everything in your life.

Like the wise men, you "sought" Jesus. You went on a search for Him. . .and you found Him! And just like the wise men, you brought Him a gift—your heart.

Pray:

Thank You, Lord, for the reminder that wise men and women are still seeking You. I didn't have to look far to find You, Father. You were there all along. I'm so grateful. Amen.

....

....

....

....

....

....

....

....

....

....

....

....

A FURNACE OF FAITH
Read Daniel 3

Key Verse:

Then King Nebuchadnezzar was astonished and rose up in haste. He declared to his counselors, "Did we not cast three men bound into the fire?" They answered and said to the king, "True, O king." He answered and said, "But I see four men unbound, walking in the midst of the fire, and they are not hurt; and the appearance of the fourth is like a son of the gods."
DANIEL 3:24–25 ESV

Understand:

- *God protected the three Hebrew children and spared their lives. Has He ever delivered you from a scary situation in a miraculous way?*
- *Who was the fourth man in the fire?*

Apply:

If you're like most people, you have a healthy fear of fire. The idea of being tossed into a fiery furnace is probably high at the top of your "Please don't ever let this happen to me, Lord" list. It's remarkable to consider the faith of Shadrach, Meshach, and Abednego as flames leaped around them.

Think of the fieriest trial you've ever walked through. In the midst of it, were you afraid the flames would take you down? Did anxieties cripple you to the point where you couldn't function? How did Jesus rush in to meet you in the middle of your trouble? Surely He has delivered you just as He did the men in the fiery furnace.

There will always be trials. We will always have opposition in this life, people like Nebuchadnezzar who think they have a right to inflict pain on us. But take heart! God will be with you, even in your darkest hour. You'll come out of every fiery trial without the smell of smoke!

Pray:

Father, I'm so relieved to know that You will stick with me, even in the fiery trials I face. I could never make it on my own. Thank You for Your ever-present help in time of trouble. Amen.

....

....

....

....

....

....

....

....

....

HAVE A LITTLE TALK WITH JESUS
Read Luke 19:1–10

Key Verse:

A man was there by the name of Zacchaeus; he was a chief tax collector and was wealthy. He wanted to see who Jesus was, but because he was short he could not see over the crowd. So he ran ahead and climbed a sycamore-fig tree to see him, since Jesus was coming that way.
LUKE 19:2–4 NIV

Understand:

- *Zacchaeus went to great lengths to have a great spot to see Jesus. Have you ever gone to great lengths to spend time with Him?*
- *Why were the people so irritated with tax collectors like Zacchaeus?*

Apply:

When you're the local tax collector (a man hated by all), and when you're a wee bit on the short side, you don't press your way through the crowd to see the Savior. You find a way to sneak up, up, up to a safe place to catch a glimpse as He passes through.

Though Zacchaeus thought he was just going to play the role of spectator that fateful day, the Lord had other ideas. Jesus stopped, pointed up to the tree, called Zacchaeus by name, and said, *"Come down! I'm going to your house today!"*

Have you ever felt shunned or unloved like Zacchaeus? Have you ever wondered how—or why—Jesus would pick someone like you to hang out with? The truth is, He adores everyone equally—the loved, the unloved, the faithful, the sinner, the whole, the broken. . .everyone. He points His finger, smiles, and says, *"Draw close! I'm going to your house today."*

Pray:

I'm grateful You want to spend time with me, Lord. I'm not exactly the most popular person in town. Sometimes I feel like I've been pushed aside, like Zacchaeus. But You welcome me into Your presence, and I'm so happy to spend time with You. Amen.

....

....

....

....

....

....

....

....

....

....

A DEN OF LIONS
Read Daniel 6

Key Verse:

"My God sent his angel, and he shut the mouths of the lions. They have not hurt me, because I was found innocent in his sight. Nor have I ever done any wrong before you, Your Majesty."
DANIEL 6:22 NIV

Understand:

- *Daniel's life was spared when God literally closed the mouths of the lions. Has He ever spared your life?*
- *Daniel was spared because he was found innocent in God's sight. What is it that makes you innocent in God's sight?*

Apply:

What a conundrum! Daniel worshipped the one true God during a time when it was illegal to do so. The king had issued a decree that anyone caught praying would be thrown into the lions' den. This did not deter Daniel. He continued to cry out to the Lord.

When he was caught praying, Daniel was tossed into the den of lions. A stone was placed over the opening of the den and sealed with the king's ring. Then a remarkable thing happened—God shut the mouths of the lions, and they didn't bother Daniel.

He lived through the ordeal.

Maybe you're walking through a situation where it's awkward or even dangerous to share your faith. Maybe someone on the job, at school, or in your community has come against you for your beliefs. You're riddled with anxiety and fear.

Do your best to walk in faith and never forget Daniel's story. God didn't rescue him from the ordeal; instead, He chose to close the mouths of the lions.

He can do that for you too. Hold your head high, cling to your faith, and then watch as God's hand of protection guards you every step of the way.

Pray:

It's not always easy to take a stand for my faith, Lord. Sometimes I wonder if my children and grandchildren will have any freedom to worship. But I won't give up. I'll keep worshipping You, no matter what. Amen.

....

....

....

....

....

....

....

....

THE BUSINESS OF CREATING
Read Genesis 1

~

Key Verse:

God saw all that he had made, and it was very good.
And there was evening, and there was
morning—the sixth day.
GENESIS 1:31 NIV

Understand:

- *God is in the business of creating! He's still creating new hearts and new situations every day. What's the most amazing thing He's created in your life?*
- *You are created in the image of your very creative Father—God. Would you consider yourself a creative person?*

Apply:

Can you even imagine being there at creation—to watch in amazement as the Creator called everything into being? With just a word, rivers ran, mountains rose, stars twinkled, and planet Earth began to spin. Giraffes' necks grew, river otters leaped off rocks into the water, and eagles soared.

Our creative God has a remarkable imagination. Who else could have come up with the kangaroo, the sloth, and fire ants in the same week? Who else could dream up hummingbirds, llamas, and armadillos without thinking twice?

His imagination was at work during creation week, but the show didn't stop there! He's still busy, creating new hearts and lives in you and those you love.

God has given you the same power to create, which is why you're able to use your imagination as you do. He's also given you the ability to come up with ideas, one after the other. Yes, God passed His imagination down to you, His child. So use it to His glory!

Pray:

Father, thank You for Your creation! I'm amazed by all the beauty surrounding me—majestic mountains, fields of wheat, and sandy shores. What a creative God You are! Thank You for placing that same creativity in me, so that my imagination runs wild. I'm so glad to be created in Your image. Amen.

....

....

....

....

....

....

....

....

....

WHERE YOU GO
Read Ruth 1

~

Key Verse:

But Ruth replied, "Don't urge me to leave you or to turn back from you. Where you go I will go, and where you stay I will stay. Your people will be my people and your God my God."
RUTH 1:16 NIV

Understand:

- *Have you ever bonded with a family member like Ruth bonded with Naomi?*
- *Would you be willing to travel with a close friend or with family to a different country to live?*

Apply:

At first glance, it would appear that Ruth and Naomi had lost everything. Both of their husbands passed away. Despair set in. But they still had one very special thing—each other. From the moment Ruth uttered those amazing words, "Where you go, I'll go. Where you stay, I'll stay," the bond was set in stone. They were in this together.

Maybe you've walked a mile in Ruth's shoes. You've lost much. Things look bleak. Anxieties have you in their grip. You're not sure where to go or what to do. But you have one thing—a relationship with a friend or loved one who won't let you walk through the valley alone. You have your Naomi.

Today, look around you. Examine your friend-ships. Likely, there's a Ruth out there, needing a Naomi, someone she can stick close to. Pray. Ask the Lord if you should sweep that young Ruth under your wing and walk her through the valley. She needs you, you know. And you need her too.

Pray:

Father, thank You for the many times You've surrounded me with just the right people. Walking through rough seasons is easier with the support of a friend or loved one. I'm so grateful for those who care, Lord. Amen.

....

....

....

....

....

....

....

....

....

....

....

MIXED MESSAGES
Read Genesis 11:1–9

Key Verse:

*That is why it was called Babel—because there the LORD
confused the language of the whole world. From there the
LORD scattered them over the face of the whole earth.*
GENESIS 11:9 NIV

Understand:

- *The world sends so many mixed messages.
  Which ones confuse you the most?*
- *Why do you suppose God chose to confuse the
  language and scatter people across the face of
  the earth?*

Apply:

Not long after Adam and Eve left the garden, an
unusual event took place. The people (who had everything in common, including their language) began to
build a tower to make a name for themselves. When
God saw what they planned to accomplish, He chose
to shake things up a bit. He confused their language
and scattered the people.

Strange, right? God is usually all about unity,
not division. Why split up the people? Why scatter
them across the globe? The truth is, these folks were
getting a little too puffed up. They were looking at
themselves as heroes, saviors. Yes, they were working

together, but only to bring glory to themselves.

Maybe you've been in a similar situation where a team effort ended up being about personal glory. Or maybe you've experienced excessive pride in a coworker or someone on a sports team. We can all get a little puffed up at times. As believers, we send a mixed message when we begin to tout ourselves instead of the Lord. It's time to refocus on Him, to take our eyes off ourselves so that He can be magnified.

Pray:

Father, I want to give all the glory to You. You're the only Savior I'll ever need. If I begin to sing my own praises, stop me, I pray. May I only live to praise You. Amen.

....

....

....

....

....

....

....

....

....

....

ALIVE!
Read Mark 16

Key Verse:

As they entered the tomb, they saw a young man dressed in a white robe sitting on the right side, and they were alarmed. "Don't be alarmed," he said. "You are looking for Jesus the Nazarene, who was crucified. He has risen! He is not here. See the place where they laid him."
MARK 16:5–6 NIV

Understand:

- *The resurrection of Jesus is one of history's most compelling events. What does it mean to you?*
- *Why would the resurrection of Jesus cause alarm?*

Apply:

If you've ever attended a funeral or visited a grave site, the last thing you expect is for the body to go missing. But that's what happened in this, the most famous death scene ever written. Jesus died on the cross and was buried in the tomb, but on the third day, He sprang back to life.

The entire Gospel story hinges on this one event: the resurrection. If Jesus hadn't risen from the grave, if His death on the cross had ended the story, would we still be celebrating Him today? The resurrection seals the deal! It shows us, His followers, that death has no hold on us. We're meant to live forever with Him. It's also proof positive that Jesus was who He said He was, the Savior of mankind. For only a Savior would rise again with power and authority. And that same authority has been given to us, His kids.

What graveclothes are holding you back today? Speak with authority over your situation and watch as resurrection power springs you from death to life.

Pray:

Thank You for the resurrection, Lord! You are exactly who You claimed to be—Messiah and King. Thank You for the authority You've given me. I want to live with resurrection power, no matter what I'm going through. Death has no victory over me. Amen!

....

....

....

....

....

....

....

....

....

....

WALK IN WISDOM
Read 1 Kings 3:16–28

⌒

Key Verse:

Solomon said, "Don't kill the baby." Then he pointed to the first woman, "She is his real mother. Give the baby to her."
1 KINGS 3:27 CEV

Understand:

- *Solomon was quick on his feet! He came up with the perfect solution to the problem, didn't he? Can you think of a time when you were quick on your feet?*
- *Where do you need the most wisdom— at home, work, or school, or with your relationships?*

Apply:

Perhaps you've heard someone say, "You have the wisdom of Solomon." Maybe you've wondered what that meant. What gave Solomon the edge wasn't just his wisdom, but his ability to discern a situation and then make decisions based on his discernment.

Two women showed up with one baby, each arguing that the baby belonged to her. How would Solomon solve the problem? In a very interesting way! He instructed them to cut the baby in half. Of course, the real mother cried out in anguish while the wannabe mom agreed to Solomon's terms. It was obvious in a flash who the real mom was.

Maybe you want the wisdom of Solomon. It's easy to acquire. The Bible tells us that we're all able to tap into that well. But while you're at it, also ask the Lord for discernment. Wisdom and discernment work hand in hand, after all.

Pray:

Lord, thank You for discernment and wisdom. I can't drum these things up on my own, but You freely give them to me when I ask. Today, I ask. Fill my cup, Lord. Amen.

....

....

....

....

....

....

....

....

....

....

....

....

....

THE DEATH OF A DREAM
Read Matthew 27:1–56

⌒

Key Verse:

*Many women were there, watching from a distance.
They had followed Jesus from Galilee to care for his needs.
Among them were Mary Magdalene, Mary the mother
of James and Joseph, and the mother of Zebedee's sons.*
MATTHEW 27:55–56 NIV

Understand:

- *How the disciples must have mourned Jesus'
  death! And not just for the obvious reasons.
  Surely they felt it meant the end of a dream.
  Have you ever watched a dream die?*
- *Is it possible to have hope in a hopeless
  situation?*

Apply:

It's easy to imagine what must have been going
through the hearts and minds of the disciples as they
watched their friend, teacher, mentor hanging on the
cross. Though Jesus had told them He would rise
again, they must've had their doubts as He breathed
His last on the cross. In that moment as heaven met
earth for the most sobering moment ever, how they
must have mourned the death of a dream. Oh, but
the joy of realizing, just a few days later, the resurrection of their hopes and dreams.

Maybe you've watched a dream die. Maybe you've given everything to see it come to pass, only to watch it slip through your fingertips. Maybe hopelessness has crept in. Today God wants you to know that He can give you hope, even when all around you seems hopeless. He wants to give you resurrection power, even in the moments when you're overwhelmed with anxieties.

Don't give up. God has great things ahead for you. This too shall pass, and you'll be on your feet and running again.

Pray:

Father, it's been painful to watch my dreams die. So many times I've felt like giving up. Thank You for the reminder that resurrection is coming! Amen.

....

....

....

....

....

....

....

....

....

PRAYER AND PETITION
Read Matthew 6:9–13

⌒

Key Verse:

*"This, then, is how you should pray:
'Our Father in heaven, hallowed be your name.'"*
MATTHEW 6:9 NIV

Understand:

- *Have you ever had to plead a case in court?
  What did it feel like, to speak before the
  judge?*
- *Isn't it wonderful to know you have instant
  access to the King of all kings, God Himself?
  What wows you the most about that idea?*

Apply:

"Our Father in heaven, hallowed be your name." We
know and love those words. They give us power and
hope. They connect us to the King of the universe
and remind us that He cares about even the smallest
of details. Our ability to converse with our Creator,
to offer our prayers and petitions, is such a privilege.

Many times, we come before the Lord with
requests that seem overwhelming. A friend has a
cancer diagnosis. A loved one has been in an accident. A friend's child has died. It's all too much to
take in. But God wants us to bring those things to
Him, to plead our case (no matter how difficult the

need), and to release the burden to Him. For only in releasing the burden can we truly walk in freedom.

What are you holding on to today? What need feels too great? What burden is too heavy? What anxieties are too unnerving? Run to the Lord. Start with the words "Our Father in heaven," and go from there. He longs for you to bare your heart.

Pray:

Our Father in heaven. . .You are an awesome and amazing God! Thank You for Your willingness to listen to my pleas and move on my behalf. I'm so glad I can cast my cares on You, Lord. Amen.

....

....

....

....

....

....

....

....

....

....

....

FOOD FOR DAYS
Read 1 Kings 17:7–16

⌒

Key Verse:

"For this is what the LORD, the God of Israel, says: 'The jar of flour will not be used up and the jug of oil will not run dry until the day the LORD sends rain on the land.'"

1 KINGS 17:14 NIV

Understand:

- *Have you ever been through a season of lack, where provisions were in short supply? What did you do?*
- *How do you garner the faith to believe for the impossible during lean seasons?*

Apply:

Imagine the plight of that poor widow woman. A child to feed. No way to replenish what little food she had in the house. And then, on top of everything, the man of God wants her to share? Must have felt impossible. And intrusive.

Now imagine how she must have felt, meal after meal, day after day, as the flour and oil replenished themselves. Surely she blinked, stared at her ingredients to make sure she wasn't losing her mind, and then blinked again. Wow!

Maybe you've been in her place. Your provisions were low. You wondered where the next meal was going to come from. From out of nowhere, a bag of groceries appeared on your doorstep. A gift card arrived from a friend. An unexpected check showed up in the mailbox.

God loves to replenish your storehouse, and His methods are always imaginative and fun. So don't fret. Don't be anxious about tomorrow. You won't go hungry. He's got this one covered.

Pray:

Thank You for Your provision, Lord. You've seen me through every lean season, making sure I had everything I needed and more. I'm so grateful. Amen.

....

....

....

....

....

....

....

....

....

....

BE HAPPY ATTITUDES
Read Matthew 5:1–12

⌒

Key Verse:

Now when Jesus saw the crowds, he went up on a mountainside and sat down. His disciples came to him, and he began to teach them.
MATTHEW 5:1–2 NIV

Understand:

- *The Beatitudes give us all we need to live a happy, fulfilled life. Which one speaks to you the most, and why?*
- *Why do you suppose God is concerned with blessing us and making sure we experience happiness in this life?*

Apply:

Have you ever wondered why Jesus took the time to deliver the Sermon on the Mount or to include the Beatitudes as part of His message? If He had skipped over them, we might never have known that we are blessed when persecuted or comforted when mourning. Maybe we'd never realize that the meek would inherit the earth or that the merciful would be shown mercy.

These few lines of scripture are filled with promises from on high. They bring hope to the hopeless and joy to the downtrodden. They remind us that any anxious thoughts can dissipate in the presence of the Lord.

Some people refer to the Beatitudes as the "be happy attitudes." When you apply them to your life, they bring peace and, ultimately, happiness.

Which beatitude are you leaning most heavily on at this point in your life? Remember, Jesus took the time to insert that line of scripture so that you would know His peace and joy.

Pray:

Thank You for shifting my attitude with these scriptures, Lord! I'm so glad You included them in Your text. You think of everything, Father. Amen.

....

....

....

....

....

....

....

....

....

....

....

A SECOND CHANCE AT LIFE
Read John 11:1–44

Key Verse:

*When he had said this, Jesus called in a loud voice,
"Lazarus, come out!" The dead man came out, his hands
and feet wrapped with strips of linen, and a cloth
around his face. Jesus said to them, "Take off
the grave clothes and let him go."*
JOHN 11:43–44 NIV

Understand:

- *Have you ever felt as if you'd been given a
second chance at life? What thrilled you the
most about tearing off the graveclothes?*
- *Picture yourself in the crowd as Lazarus
burst forth from the tomb. What would you be
thinking or doing?*

Apply:

Most people look at death as the end of a story.
When the last breath is taken, the story has come to
its conclusion. The opposite is true with God! At the
point of death, things are just getting started! We've got
the promise of heaven and life eternal—complete with
mansions, streets of gold, and pearly gates.

In the story of Lazarus, however, Jesus decided to
change things up a bit. He decided that heaven could
wait a little longer for this man of faith. In front of a

crowd of witnesses, Jesus cried out, *"Lazarus, come forth!"* The man who had been wrapped in graveclothes for days came out of his tomb and shocked the crowd as he moved toward them. Can you even imagine?

Lazarus was given a second chance at life (though he probably would have preferred heaven). This gift was as much, if not more, for his family and friends, who missed him terribly. Maybe you can relate on a much smaller scale. Maybe you've been given a second chance, a fresh breath. You shocked the doctors when you recovered from a near-death experience. You missed being in an accident by inches. You survived a heart-wrenching breakup. Your graveclothes have now been stripped away, and you're free to begin again.

What will you do with this second chance? How will you live this next phase of your life? Come bursting forth, as Lazarus did, ready to face a new day.

Pray:

Lord, You are a God of second chances. I've experienced this in my life so many times, and I'm so grateful. Today I burst forth from the tomb, ready for new adventures. Thank You, Lord. Amen.

....

....

....

....

....

THE BELLY OF THE WHALE
Read Jonah 1–2

⌒

Key Verse:

From inside the fish Jonah prayed to the LORD his God.
He said: "In my distress I called to the LORD, and he
answered me. From deep in the realm of the dead
I called for help, and you listened to my cry."
JONAH 2:1–2 NIV

Understand:

- *Jonah's disobedience had consequences. He landed in the belly of a whale. Has your disobedience ever landed you in an awkward place?*
- *What do you suppose Jonah was thinking while inside the fish?*

Apply:

Jonah didn't want to go to Nineveh. It's as plain and simple as that. He knew that confronting the Ninevites about their sinful condition would likely result in kickback. (After all, who wants to be reminded of their wickedness?) So he ran in the opposite direction. As a result, he found himself in a jam, one unlike any other in history before or after.

Chances are pretty good you've never landed inside the belly of a fish, but you've probably walked through rebellious seasons where your disobedience resulted in harsh consequences. Like Jonah, you were trapped in a prison of your own creation.

God loves it when He's got our full, undivided attention. No matter where you're sitting, He longs to speak to you, to give guidance and direction. Whether you're in a prison cell, a quiet bedroom, or the belly of a fish.

No running in the opposite direction! Even if His instructions are difficult, God will give you everything you need, as long as you stay on the right path. Otherwise, you might just end up in a place you really don't want to be.

Pray:

I'll admit it, Lord. . .sometimes I run. I do the opposite of what You ask me to do. I let fear get the best of me. Then I suffer the consequences. Today, give me the courage to do all You ask, that I might live in safety.
I trust You, Father. Amen.

....
....
....
....
....
....
....
....

THAT KIND OF FRIEND
Read Luke 5:17–39

$\frown$

Key Verse:

*But they could not find a way to take him in because
of so many people. They made a hole in the roof over
where Jesus stood. Then they let the bed with
the sick man on it down before Jesus.*

LUKE 5:19 NLV

Understand:

- *This story fits the phrase "Desperate times call
  for desperate measures." Have you ever been
  desperate to lead a friend to Jesus (for healing
  or salvation)?*
- *Why did the Pharisees panic when Jesus
  forgave the man for his sins?*

Apply:

Let's face it—whenever a large crowd gathers, it's hard
to break through. The friends of the man in this story
had that part figured out. So they concocted a plan.
They climbed up on the roof of the house above the
spot where Jesus was speaking. Then they cut a hole in
the roof and lowered their sick friend (who was still
on his cot) into the room, right where Jesus was.

Talk about an interruption! Jesus was likely in
the middle of teaching, preaching, or performing
miracles when this fellow came floating down

from the sky above.

It really touches the heart to see just how much these friends cared. They would move heaven and earth to see their sick friend healed.

Maybe you have friends like that. They've rallied around you during a tough season. Or maybe you've been that sort of friend to others. Everyone needs a friend who will go to bat for them.

Jesus stopped everything to heal this man. And He will stop everything to meet your needs as well. What do you need today?

Pray:

Thank You for the reminder that You will stop everything to meet my need, Lord. I want to be the kind of friend who will do that for those I love. Keep my eyes wide open as I look over my friends list, Lord. Amen.

....

....

....

....

....

....

....

....

....

COME, HOLY SPIRIT
Read Acts 2:1–41

Key Verse:

When the day of Pentecost came, they were all together in one place. Suddenly a sound like the blowing of a violent wind came from heaven and filled the whole house where they were sitting.
ACTS 2:1–2 NIV

Understand:

- *What a remarkable day! The day of Pentecost changed everything. Have you ever been in a church service or gathering where the Holy Spirit's presence was this overpowering?*
- *How do you respond to the tangible, powerful presence of the Holy Spirit?*

Apply:

This amazing story begins with a powerful, important sentence: "When the day of Pentecost came, they were all together in one place." Jesus' followers were waiting with great anticipation in the upper room. . . together. They were united—in spirit, in the flesh, even in their way of thinking. Their unity provided the perfect environment for the Holy Spirit to show up. . .and show off!

God's powerful presence on the day of Pentecost still stirs the hearts of believers everywhere. What happened to Jesus' followers on that amazing day remains a key topic of discussion in churches around the world, two thousand years later.

When the Holy Spirit rushes into a situation, everything changes! Weakness is replaced with strength. Depression has to give way to joy. Confusion is swapped out for clear thinking. More than anything, the presence of the Holy Spirit invigorates and encourages us and reminds us of one critical fact: God is still right here, with us. He hasn't left us and never will. What peace and comfort that brings!

Pray:

Come, Holy Spirit! How we need Your presence. We need healing, joy, restoration. We need the reminder that God is for us, with us, and in us. Come, Holy Spirit, we pray. Amen.

....

....

....

....

....

....

....

....

....

THE ANCHOR HOLDS
Read Acts 27:27–28:5

$\sim$

Key Verse:

*But the ship struck a sandbar and ran aground.
The bow stuck fast and would not move, and the stern
was broken to pieces by the pounding of the surf.*
ACTS 27:41 NIV

Understand:

- *What a remarkable man Paul was! Even
  when shipwrecked, he didn't lose his faith.
  Can you imagine being washed up on the
  shore of a desert island? How would this
  affect your faith?*
- *Sometimes our faith feels shipwrecked. Think
  of a time when you felt like that.*

Apply:

If you made a list of all the things you hoped would
never happen to you, "shipwreck" might be high
on the list. No one ever thinks they'll go through
such an unusual tragedy. Likely, Paul didn't think he
would either. But that's exactly the position he found
himself in as the ship he was on struck a sandbar and
ran aground. In that moment, he had two choices:
panic, or be present in the situation.

Because Paul knew that God had his back, he
remained present in the situation. He never lost his

faith. In fact, he stood before the other men and encouraged them to find their courage.

Maybe you relate more to the other men on the ship. Maybe you're more inclined to panic in an emergency. Instead, do your best to follow Paul's lead. Stand firm. Remember, the anchor (Jesus) holds steady, even when winds and waves are tossing you to and fro. Don't let your faith be shipwrecked. Hold tight to the anchor and you'll live to face another day.

Pray:

Thank You for holding steady, Jesus! I will remain present in the situation because I know You've got me covered. Praise You! Amen.

....
....
....
....
....
....
....
....
....
....
....

A PICNIC OF FAITH
Read Matthew 14:13–21

Key Verse:

They all ate and were satisfied, and the disciples picked up twelve basketfuls of broken pieces that were left over.
MATTHEW 14:20 NIV

Understand:

- *It took the faith of a child to feed five thousand people that memorable day. Have you ever had to exhibit childlike faith in order to see a miracle take place?*
- *Has God ever performed a "loaves and fishes" miracle in your finances?*

Apply:

How we love this story of Jesus feeding the five thousand. It reminds us that He has the ability to take our "little" and turn it into a lot. It's also a great reminder that God is our Provider. Even when it looks like the cupboard is bare, He's got the ability to fill it in His own miraculous way.

A key player in this story is the young boy who offered up his lunch. If he hadn't let go of what was rightfully his, the others would have gone without. Think about that for a moment. There are times when God asks us to give up the "good" so that He can multiply it and give it back to us as the "best."

Where do you stand today? Are you in need of a "loaves and fishes" miracle? Are you riddled with anxiety while you wait? Then open your hands and get ready to let go of what you've been clinging to. Sure, it might take courage, but when you see God's plan to multiply what you've given Him, you'll be astounded!

Pray:

There have been seasons in my life, Lord, when I've doubted Your provision. I've looked inside my near-empty picnic basket and panicked. Thank You for the reminder that You can multiply anything I offer You. May I never forget how much You care. Amen.

....

....

....

....

....

....

....

....

....

....

....

THE HANDWRITING'S ON THE WALL
Read Daniel 5:1–30

Key Verse:

Suddenly the fingers of a human hand appeared and wrote on the plaster of the wall, near the lampstand in the royal palace. The king watched the hand as it wrote. His face turned pale and he was so frightened that his legs became weak and his knees were knocking.
DANIEL 5:5–6 NIV

Understand:

- *God speaks in numerous ways, but you've likely never seen Him write on a wall. What's the most unusual way God has spoken to your heart?*
- *Why do you suppose God chose this particular way to speak to the king?*

Apply:

Throughout history, God has chosen a number of ways to speak to His kids: by appearing in a fiery bush for Moses, by knocking walls down around Jericho for Joshua, by providing a ram in the thicket for Abraham, by providing a child for Hannah. He even used a donkey to speak to Balaam. He's very creative!

Perhaps one of the most unusual ways God ever spoke was through the handwriting on the wall in this story from Daniel. Can you even imagine the terror as a human hand appeared and started to write on the wall, right in front of you? Which would be more important, do you think—what was written, or who was behind the message?

Maybe God has spoken in unusual ways in your life—through circumstances, through a friend, through a sermon, or through a particular scripture passage from the Bible. There are numerous ways God can speak to a heart. Keep your eyes and ears open. He's got a lot to say, and you don't want to miss a thing.

Pray:

You're so creative, Lord! You can speak in any way
You choose. I will be listening, I promise.
So speak to my heart, I pray. Amen.

....

....

....

....

....

....

....

....

....

WATER INTO WINE
Read John 2:1–12

Key Verse:

"A host always serves the best wine first," he said.
"Then, when everyone has had a lot to drink,
he brings out the less expensive wine.
But you have kept the best until now!"
JOHN 2:10 NLT

Understand:

- *Why do you suppose the line about the best wine being served first matters in this story?*
- *Have you ever wondered why Jesus chose to perform His first public miracle at a wedding?*

Apply:

All the Gospels give us insight into the life of Jesus, starting with His childhood and moving into His ministry years. At thirty years of age, Jesus found Himself at a wedding. The host ran out of wine (a cultural no-no). Jesus' mother came to Him to ask a favor, "Son, do you think you could. . ."

Jesus' first response was to tell her that the time had not come. Then, after thinking it through, He performed His very first miracle—turning water into wine.

There's a lot of debate about why His first miracle

took place at a wedding, and why He chose turning water into wine. Some would argue that a miraculous healing (restoring sight to the blind, causing deaf ears to hear) might have been more impressive.

But Jesus chose to perform an "everyday" miracle, one that shows us He cares about the little things—when the faucet is leaking, when the car breaks down, when the refrigerator stops working. You can cry out to Him, even in the everyday things, and He's ready with a miracle. What a loving Savior we have.

Pray:

I'm glad You care about the details, Lord. I can go to You with every concern, every problem. If You took the time to bless a wedding host and his guests, I know You will meet my every need. Amen.

....

....

....

....

....

....

....

....

....

SIT AT HIS FEET
Read Matthew 19:1–15

❧

Key Verse:

Then the people brought their little children to Jesus so he could put his hands on them and pray for them. His followers told them to stop, but Jesus said, "Let the little children come to me. Don't stop them, because the kingdom of heaven belongs to people who are like these children."
MATTHEW 19:13–14 NCV

Understand:

- *Why do you think Jesus has such a special place in His heart for children?*
- *Have you ever felt like a child, sitting at Jesus' feet?*

Apply:

It's so interesting to note that the disciples made an assumption that Jesus wouldn't want the children to gather close around Him. Why do you suppose that was? Perhaps they found it culturally unacceptable. Maybe they felt He had bigger, more important things to do. But Jesus put all those disciples in their place with these words: *"Let the little children come to me. Don't stop them, because the kingdom of heaven belongs to people who are like these children."*

Don't you love that? Jesus wants the children. He loves the little children. They aren't an annoyance to

Him. On the contrary, those babes bring great joy and delight to His heart.

The Bible says that God wants us to come to Him as a little child—with childlike faith and innocence. So run to Him today. Don't worry about what others around you might be saying. Ignore their protests and curl up at Jesus' feet. Release those anxieties. Listen to the cadence of His voice. Feel the joy that radiates from every word.

He loves you, you know—no matter your age. And He wants to spend time with you today.

Pray:

Jesus, You love the little children! It's more than just a song. You love all the children of the world—every age, every color, every race. Today I come to You with the faith of a child. My heart is wide open, ready to hear what You have to say. Amen.

....

....

....

....

....

....

....

....

RESTING IN HIM
Read Luke 10:38–42

⌒

Key Verse:

*She had a sister called Mary, who sat at the
Lord's feet listening to what he said.*
LUKE 10:39 NIV

Understand:

- *Martha wasn't a bad woman. She was
  simply busy. Have you ever been so busy that
  you pushed your time with the Lord aside?*
- *Mary chose the better path—sitting at Jesus'
  feet, listening to Him as He ministered. Why
  do you think God prefers her approach to
  Martha's?*

Apply:

Let's face it, life can get crazy at times. We've got to
get the kids to school, then off to Little League, bal-
let class, piano lessons, and so on. On top of this we
have bills to pay, appliance repairmen to call, and a
job to get to. At the end of the day we drop into bed,
completely exhausted. Somewhere, in the middle of
it all, we have to make sure the dishes are washed, the
floors swept, and the laundry folded. Whew! Talk
about exhausting!

Surely Martha understood this sort of chaotic,
anxiety-driven lifestyle. She was a workaholic too.

And Jesus (who has nothing against workaholics, by the way) saw her exhaustion. He pointed to her sister Mary, who had chosen to recline at His feet, and asked Martha to consider resting awhile too.

Maybe you're more Martha than Mary. You have a hard time stopping. You just keep going, going, going, even if it means giving up your quiet time with the Lord. Today He's calling out to you, begging you to cease your labors for a moment and rest at His feet. What have you got to lose? Take a load off and sit for a while.

Pray:

Father, thank You for the reminder that I need to rest.
Sometimes I overdo it. Okay, most of the time I overdo it.
But I will do my best to be more Mary than Martha
today, no matter what I'm facing. Amen.

....

....

....

....

....

....

....

....

....

BROTHERLY LOVE
Read 1 Samuel 18

Key Verse:

Then Jonathan made a covenant with David,
because he loved him as his own soul.
1 SAMUEL 18:3 ESV

Understand:

- *Can you remember the name of your earliest childhood friend? What drew you to this person? Are you still in touch?*
- *Why does God care so much about our relationships with others?*

Apply:

Have you ever had a friend who was so close you were practically the same person? You laughed alike, talked alike, sometimes even dressed alike. That's how Jonathan and David were. These two BFFs were inseparable. Where one went, the other would follow. The boys grew up together and, as boys are wont to do, probably got into lots of mischief together. As they grew, they became mutual protectors in the game of life. The words "He's got my back" were surely their motto.

Maybe you've had a friend like that. The two of you did everything together. Good, bad, indifferent... as a duo you could handle anything. Chaos, laughs, tears. . .you bonded over anything and everything.

When you find a friend like that, you've found a real treasure.

The world focuses so much on romantic love but very little on friendship. The Bible, however, highlights friendships such as the one between Jonathan and David so that we never forget—brotherly love is critical to our survival. We were created for relationships, after all.

Pray:

Lord, I'm so thankful for brotherly love. I don't know where I'd be without the close friendships I've had over the years. I'm so grateful, Father. Amen.

....

....

....

....

....

....

....

....

....

....

....

WHEN TIME STANDS STILL
Read Joshua 10:1–28

Key Verse:

On the day that the LORD gave up the Amorites to the Israelites, Joshua stood before all the people of Israel and said to the LORD: "Sun, stand still over Gibeon. Moon, stand still over the Valley of Aijalon." So the sun stood still, and the moon stopped until the people defeated their enemies. These words are written in the Book of Jashar. The sun stopped in the middle of the sky and waited to go down for a full day. That has never happened at any time before that day or since. That was the day the LORD listened to a human being. Truly the LORD was fighting for Israel!
JOSHUA 10:12–14 NCV

Understand:

- *"That was the day the LORD listened to a human being." What do those words mean to you?*
- *Is God listening to you? If so, how does He respond to your requests?*

Apply:

This has to be one of the most fascinating stories in the Bible. Rarely do we stumble across a tale where a human called the shots and God obeyed. It's not that Joshua was bossing God around. He simply took the time to understand God's will and then just spoke with authority as he called the sun and moon to stand still. Might sound like he was a know-it-all, but that's not the case.

Did you know that God likes it when you speak with authority? When you look the enemy in the eye and say, "Be gone in Jesus' name!" you're actually speaking His Word, His truth over the situation. And, like Joshua, you'll see miracles happen as a result.

Pray:

Thank You for the reminder that I can speak with authority, even in the midst of the battle, Lord. I want to see miracles, just like Joshua did. Amen.

....

....

....

....

....

....

....

....

....

....

....

....

....

A RAINBOW OF PROMISE
Read Genesis 9:1–17

⌒

Key Verse:

"I am putting my rainbow in the clouds as the sign of the agreement between me and the earth."
GENESIS 9:13 NCV

Understand:

- *Have you ever reached the end of a long journey to find a rainbow of hope at the end?*
- *Why do you suppose God chose to use all the colors of the rainbow to signify hope?*

Apply:

There are a variety of stories in the Old Testament where God made a covenant with man. Nearly every famous Bible character had some sort of encounter that would fall into this category. For Noah, however, the covenant was very unusual.

After the ark came to a halt on Mount Ararat, a rainbow filled the sky. Clearly, Noah, his wife, his sons, and his daughters-in-law had never seen anything like it. How they must have marveled at the arc of color, shimmering in the sky above. Can you imagine the oohing and aahing?

God promised that He would never again destroy the earth with floodwaters, and He "covenanted" that promise by setting the rainbow in the sky.

Has God made any promises to you? How has He sealed those promises? Does He remind you in the middle of the storms, so that you won't give up? He's not a promise breaker, after all.

Pray:

Father, I'm so glad You're a promise keeper! If You said it, I know You'll follow through. I'm grateful for the covenants You've made with me, Lord. You are worthy of my praise. Amen.

....

....

....

....

....

....

....

....

....

....

....

....

....

THE GREATEST OF THESE IS LOVE
Read 1 Corinthians 13

⌒

Key Verse:

So these three things continue forever: faith, hope, and love. And the greatest of these is love.
1 CORINTHIANS 13:13 NCV

Understand:

- *Why do you suppose God went to the trouble to let us know that love is greater than any other trait we might have?*
- *When God says that faith, hope, and love continue forever, what does He mean?*

Apply:

Perhaps there is no chapter in the Bible quoted more often than "the love chapter." You hear 1 Corinthians 13 most often at weddings. Love is the greatest of all the gifts. We read that, nod, and say, "Sure. I get it." But do we?

If love supersedes all, then we have to share it, even when we don't feel like it. When the neighbor's dog digs a hole under the fence. . .again. When the woman in the parking lot rams into your car. When the clerk at the supermarket double-charges you for something but doesn't want to make it right.

Love has to show up in every relationship, every encounter, every disagreement, every bump in the road. When you offer it to others, you're truly offering them the greatest gift.

Is love leading the way in your life today?

Pray:

Lord, thank You for the reminder that love needs to lead the way. So often, I let my emotions get the best of me. I struggle to show love. When I don't feel it, Father, will You please love through me? Only then can I be a true reflection of You. Amen.

....
....
....
....
....
....
....
....
....
....
....
....
....
....

THE WAIT IS ON
Read Acts 1

Read Acts 1

Key Verse:

Once when he was eating with them, he told them not to leave Jerusalem. He said, "Wait here to receive the promise from the Father which I told you about. John baptized people with water, but in a few days you will be baptized with the Holy Spirit."
ACTS 1:4–5 NCV

Understand:

- *Jesus instructed His followers to wait on the promise of the Holy Spirit. Has God ever asked you to wait on a particular promise? Are you good at waiting?*
- *The disciples were "in one accord" on the day of Pentecost. What is the importance of being in one accord with fellow believers as you wait on God to move in a miraculous way?*

Apply:

Wait. Oh, how we hate that word. In this modern age, everything is instant, from popcorn to fast food to social media posts. Even our cars come with buttons to turn them on before we get inside. We don't want to wait on a thing.

Need that check deposited in the bank quickly? Do a mobile deposit. Need to sign a document to buy a home? E-sign it. Need a recommendation for a plumber? You'll find one online in seconds. Pretty much anything you need is at your fingertips.

Because we've gotten used to the notion that things should be instant, we forget that God often calls us to wait. Like the disciples in Jerusalem, we have to tarry. It's not just a matter of physically waiting. We must change our thinking. Instead of demanding instant gratification from God, we should praise Him during the waiting period.

What are you waiting on right now? Do you have a sense of urgency? If so, relax. Let those anxieties go. God's got this. The wait will be behind you soon. In the meantime, be found faithful.

Pray:

Lord, I'm sorry for my impatience! I've been demanding with You in the past, but those days are behind me now. I want to be found faithful in the waiting, Father. Help me, I pray. Amen.

....

....

....

....

....

....

....

A GREATER PLAN
Read Exodus 2:1–10

⌒

Key Verse:

Then Pharaoh's daughter went down to the Nile to bathe, and her attendants were walking along the riverbank. She saw the basket among the reeds and sent her female slave to get it. She opened it and saw the baby. He was crying, and she felt sorry for him. "This is one of the Hebrew babies," she said.
EXODUS 2:5–6 NIV

Understand:

- *Moses' mother took a great risk, placing her baby in a basket in the river. What if things had gone a different direction? What other outcomes might have occurred?*
- *Moses would have led a completely different life if Pharaoh's daughter hadn't taken him in. Has your life ever changed because of someone's intervention?*

Apply:

Oh, the things a mother will do for her child! Moses' mom was no different from any other when it came to protecting her own. But, because of the times she lived in, desperate measures were called for. In order to keep her baby, she had to give him up. God honored her plan, and Moses' life was spared.

We live in a similar age, where Christian parents

often have to go to great extremes to protect the innocence of their children. Temptations abound, vying for a child's heart and mind. Everything from TV to video games to cell phones grabs their attention from a young age.

God has a greater plan for your child than you can imagine. So do all you can to protect him from the temptations of this life. Make sure he's safe and strong. Yes, sacrifices will have to be made. But giving your child the best possible upbringing is worth all the trouble. That's what love does, after all. . .it sacrifices.

Pray:

Thank You for the reminder that children need to be guarded and protected, Lord. I don't want the little ones in my world to succumb to temptations. Help me lead and guide, Father. Amen.

....

....

....

....

....

....

....

....

A CHANCE ENCOUNTER
Read Genesis 24

⌒

Key Verse:

*They prayed that good would come to Rebekah, and said
to her, "You are our sister. May you become the mother of
millions. May your children and all their children's children
after them take over the cities of those who hate them."
Then Rebekah and her servants got up on the camels
and followed the man. So the servant of
Abraham took Rebekah and left.*
GENESIS 24:60–61 NLV

Understand:

- *Chance encounters. . .or divine appointments? Which would you call them?*
- *Has God ever given you an amazing, life-changing encounter with a total stranger? How did that play out?*

Apply:

When Rebekah showed up at the well to draw water,
she never expected to walk away engaged to a complete stranger. She was simply doing what she always
did at that time of day. God interrupted her plans
and led her directly into the path of Abraham's servant, who was there on a mission.

The Lord led the way in this story, giving Abraham's servant specific instructions about the young

woman he was to bring back to Isaac. In Rebekah, the servant found everything he was looking for and more.

This story is an amazing reminder that God is in the details. He's also the King of divine appointments. He knows how to time things perfectly so that you're in just the right place at just the right time.

The next time you have a "chance" encounter, remember. . .God's in the details.

Pray:

Thank You for the many divine appointments in my life, Lord. I love those little "setups." What a fun, adventurous Father You are! Amen.

....

....

....

....

....

....

....

....

....

....

A BETTER CHOICE
Read Genesis 3

⌒

Key Verse:

When the woman saw that the tree was good for food, and that it was pleasant to the eyes, and a tree to be desired to make one wise, she took of the fruit thereof, and did eat, and gave also unto her husband with her; and he did eat.
GENESIS 3:6 KJV

Understand:

- *Eve saw that the tree was good for food, so she took the fruit. . .even though God had told her not to. She let something that looked good outweigh God's best. Have you ever done that?*

- *When we deliberately choose to disobey, what are the consequences?*

Apply:

Life is filled with choices. We make dozens of them a day. Will we get out of bed when the alarm goes off? What shoes will we wear today? What clothes? Should we eat breakfast or skip it? Do we drop off the kids at school or make them ride the bus? Do we start the slow cooker before leaving for work or pick up fast food on the way home this evening?

These are just a few of the choices we make.

Of course, there are bigger choices too: Who

will we marry? How many children should we have? Where will we live?

The biggest choice we'll ever make, though, is far more important than any of these: Will we give our heart to Jesus Christ and make Him Lord of our life?

Following God is the best choice we could ever make. And listening to His voice as we move forward from day to day is critical for our survival. Eve wanted to walk in relationship with God in the garden, but she wanted to have it her way too. She made a poor choice, one that had devastating consequences for mankind. May we learn from her mistake so we're not destined to repeat it.

Pray:

Father, I want to make good choices! I long to have a solid relationship with You, so I'll listen for Your still, small voice. Give me clear instructions so that I can follow hard and fast after You, Lord. Amen.

....

....

....

....

....

....

....

WALKING IN FAITH
Read Matthew 1:18–25

⁓

Key Verse:

*When Joseph woke up, he did what the Lord's angel had
told him to do. Joseph took Mary as his wife, but he did
not have sexual relations with her until she gave
birth to the son. And Joseph named him Jesus.*
MATTHEW 1:24–25 NCV

Understand:

- *Can you imagine what Joseph was going
  through? Which would be the hardest pill
  to swallow?*
- *How do you think Joseph felt whenever
  someone would say something like, "That's
  a great boy you've got there!"?*

Apply:

Joseph was a key player in the story of the birth of the
Messiah, but he's often overlooked. Mary we remember. The shepherds in the field? We'll never forget the
role they played. The angels? Who else could have
made the heavenly proclamation? The wise men,
traveling from afar to bring gifts? We are amazed at
their journey and their offerings. But when it comes
to Joseph—the man who would become dad to baby
Jesus—we often forget to mention him.

Joseph had one of the hardest jobs of all. Not only

was his reputation at stake (the gossips were surely having a field day), but he had to tackle those weird "This isn't really my son" feelings after the birth. More than anything, Joseph was asked to do something no one had ever been asked to do before—protect his pregnant virgin's image and give her baby a good home. (Try explaining that one to the grandparents-to-be.)

Without Joseph, the plan would have crumbled. Aren't you glad he stepped up and obeyed God? It took a significant amount of faith to believe the angel's instructions, but he did...and the story had a beautiful ending as a result.

Pray:

What amazing faith Joseph must have had, Lord! I'm so glad he responded to the call You placed on his life. Otherwise, the story might have had a very different ending. I want to have that kind of faith, Lord. Amen.

....

....

....

....

....

....

....

....

FLAWED BUT USABLE
Read Joshua 2

⌒

Key Verse:

The house Rahab lived in was built on the city wall,
so she used a rope to let the men down through a window.
She said to them, "Go into the hills so the king's men
will not find you. Hide there for three days. After the
king's men return, you may go on your way."
JOSHUA 2:15–16 NCV

Understand:

- *God can use anyone to accomplish great and*
  mighty things. Think of a time when He used
  an unexpected person to bless you.
- *Have you ever walked through a season*
  where you felt unusable?

Apply:

When you think of the heroes of faith, the great men
and women of the Bible, what names come to mind?
Moses? Abraham? David? Esther? Deborah? Paul?
Peter? Timothy? There are so many you could list,
but you would likely overlook one very important
and unusual one—Rahab, the harlot.

Now, it's not typical to see the name of a prosti-
tute in the lineup of biblical greats, but Rahab made
the cut because she selflessly aided the people of
God when they needed help. She risked everything

to protect them. And while many might have judged her, the Lord saw her heart.

The same is true today. There are many amazing people out there. Some might not dress like you or look like you. Others might still be trapped in a sinful lifestyle. But God loves them and longs for restoration. So take the time to talk to the Rahabs in your world. Show them that they have value, worth. You never know—God might just use that person to minister to you in ways you never expected.

Pray:

Lord, I'm so grateful that You choose to use everyone—flaws, warts, and all. May I never forget that You came for us all and love us all. I praise You, Father. Amen.

....

....

....

....

....

....

....

....

....

....

WRITTEN ON THE HEART
Read Romans 2:12–16

⌒

Key Verse:

They show that the work of the law is written on their hearts, while their conscience also bears witness, and their conflicting thoughts accuse or even excuse them on that day when, according to my gospel, God judges the secrets of men by Christ Jesus.
ROMANS 2:15–16 ESV

Understand:

- *If you've ever been in a legalistic church or relationship, you know how tough it can be to break free. Where do legalists get it wrong?*
- *How has God written His law on your heart?*

Apply:

Old Testament believers didn't have the benefit of a Savior. They were operating under the Mosaic law, laid down in the book of Leviticus. This law gave regulations for *every* aspect of life. No matter what you were going through, there was a law for it. Only one problem—no one could actually follow those laws to a tee.

Enter Jesus, the fulfillment of the law. He came to do what the law could not—save us. When we accept Him as Lord and Savior, His sacrifice on the cross covers every law we've ever broken. Best of all, when we walk in relationship with Him, He writes the law on our hearts (meaning, He takes the positive attributes of the law, mixes them up with grace, mercy, and forgiveness—and pencils them on our hearts).

Gone are the days of legalism. No more slaps on the hand for messing up. Now we long to serve Him and live by His precepts out of a deep, abiding love for Him. What a remarkable plan!

Pray:

Lord, thank You for writing Your laws on my heart. I could never keep up with all the Levitical laws, Father. I would fall short at every turn. But You sent Your Son and redeemed me from the curse of the law so that I might live in freedom. How can I ever thank You, Lord?
Praise You for the cross! Amen.

....
....
....
....
....
....
....
....
....

A STRONG FOUNDATION
Read Matthew 7

~

Key Verse:

"Everyone then who hears these words of mine and does them will be like a wise man who built his house on the rock. And the rain fell, and the floods came, and the winds blew and beat on that house, but it did not fall, because it had been founded on the rock."
MATTHEW 7:24–25 ESV

Understand:

- *A good foundation is key. Think of a time in your life when you entered into a project or situation that wasn't well founded. How did that project end?*
- *Why do you suppose God cares so much about foundations?*

Apply:

"The wise man built his house upon the rock. The foolish man built his house upon the sand." Maybe you sang those words in Sunday school, as millions of children did. Perhaps the words conjured up images of houses along the seashore, the sandy-bottomed ones cratering from within.

God has always been in the foundations business. He wants us to be rooted and founded in Him, as unmoving as a house built on stone. This can only happen if we stay in His Word and spend time with Him, growing and worshipping.

Would you say that your foundation is strong? Have you made it a point to pour into the foundations of others? Or are you content to watch them float along, like a house on shifting sand? If your "home" is in need of a new foundation, today's the day. Go back to basics. Read the Gospel of John and go from there. Ask God to rebuild you from the foundation up.

Pray:

I want to have a solid foundation, Lord. I don't want to shift to and fro with each passing wind. If there are unstable areas of my life, shore them up, I pray. Rebuild me from the foundation up, Lord. May I stand tall and strong for You! Amen.

....

....

....

....

....

....

....

....

....

UNFAIR CIRCUMSTANCES
Read Genesis 39

Key Verse:

*But the LORD was with Joseph in the prison and
showed him his faithful love. And the LORD made
Joseph a favorite with the prison warden.*
GENESIS 39:21 NLT

Understand:

- *Poor Joseph! So many unfair things happened
to him. And yet, he prevailed! Have you ever
been in an unfair situation? How did you
respond?*
- *Joseph rose to an elevated position, even while
in prison. What can you learn from his story?*

Apply:

When you read a story like Joseph's, you start to
wonder why God allowed him to go through so
much anguish. Tossed into a pit. Sold into slavery
by his brothers. Falsely accused. Banished to prison
for a crime he did not commit. That poor guy had to
jump a lot of hurdles to keep going.

Maybe you've walked a mile in Joseph's shoes.
You've been falsely accused. Those you thought you
could trust turned against you. They made your life
more difficult than it needed to be.

Here's the truth: Even when faced with the

roughest circumstances, God won't give up on you. If He could take a man like Joseph and elevate him to a position of authority in the prison, then He can take care of you, right where you are. Whatever you're struggling with today, whatever anxieties have held you in their grip, know that God won't leave you on your own. He will give you all you need, even on your hardest day.

Pray:

Lord, there have been a lot of "unfair" moments in my life so far. Far too many to count. I don't want to lose hope, Lord. I don't want to give in to anxiety. Today I give those concerns to You and choose to remain hopeful, even when circumstances have me down. Amen.

....

....

....

....

....

....

....

....

....

....

WORSHIP AT THE THRONE
Read Revelation 4

～

Key Verse:

*"Worthy are you, our Lord and God, to receive glory
and honor and power, for you created all things,
and by your will they existed and were created."*
REVELATION 4:11 ESV

Understand:

- *A day is coming when we will worship at His
  throne with no distractions, no complications,
  no pain. What are you most looking forward
  to, when you think of that day?*
- *We don't have to wait until we're in heaven
  to pour out our praises to the Lord. When you
  think of the phrase "worship with abandon,"
  what comes to mind?*

Apply:

What a spectacular picture the book of Revelation
paints of the elders worshipping around the throne!
Can't you see it now?

Do you picture yourself worshipping alongside
them? Are you surrounded by people from every
nation, tribe, and tongue? Is the song of worship in
one heavenly language or a thousand earthly ones?
Does anyone care that hours are passing by as the
songs lift and rise then shift to a new chorus?

The truth is, heaven is going to be an amazing place of worship. For there, with all distractions laid aside, we will finally be free to pour out praise uninhibited. Will you sing? Dance? Lift your hands? Only time will tell. But why wait? Let your praises begin right here, right now.

Pray:

Lord, I don't want to wait until I'm in heaven to lift a song of praise to You. You're worthy of my praise, even in this very moment, Lord. So I praise You! I sing a song of adoration in honor of the King of all kings. Bless You, my Savior! Amen.

....

....

....

....

....

....

....

....

....

....

....

....

ABOUT THE AUTHOR

Janice Thompson lives in the Houston area and writes novels, nonfiction, magazine articles, and musical comedies for the stage. The mother of four married daughters, she is quickly adding grand-children to the family mix.

ONLY HAVE 5 MINUTES? TRY THIS!

The 5-Minute Bible Study for Women

In just 5 minutes, you will *Read* (minute 1–2),
Understand (minute 3), *Apply* (minute 4), and *Pray*
(minute 5) God's Word through meaningful,
focused Bible study. *The 5-Minute Bible Study for
Women* includes more than 90 readings that
will speak to your heart in a powerful way.

Paperback / 978-1-68322-656-7 / $5.99